The Widower and the Washer

The Widower and the Washer

A MEMOIR

JAC FILER

Printed in the United States of America
Published in Hellertown, PA
Cover design by Anna Magruder
Cover Images by Serferis
Library of Congress Control Number 2025910428
ISBN 979-8-89420-052-1
For more information or to place bulk orders,
contact the author or the publisher at Jennifer@
BrightCommunications.net.

To the memory of my loving wife, Angela, faithful
partner in the koinonia of our marriage
August 28, 1983 – February 12, 2024

Contents

I thank my God every time I remember you.
In all my prayers for all of you,
I always pray with joy because of your
partnership in the gospel from the first day
until now, being confident of this, that he
who began a good work in you will carry
it on to completion until the day of Christ
Jesus.
It is right for me to feel this way
about all of you, since I have you in my
heart and, whether I am in chains or
defending and confirming the gospel, all of
you share in God's grace with me. God can
testify how I long for all of you
with the affection of Christ Jesus.
And this is my prayer: that your love
may abound more and more in knowledge
and depth of insight, so that you may be
able to discern what is best and may be pure
and blameless for the day of Christ, filled
with the fruit of righteousness that comes
through Jesus Christ—to the glory
and praise of God.
—Philippians 1:3-11

Introduction

A book about laundry?

I had the same question, but when you are a Christian writer, you don't always get to select your topics. Instead, you write what God gives you, and He gave me some interesting experiences with laundry.

The first such experience came just days after my wife, Angela, unexpectedly entered into victory. It was such a memorable scene that I turned it into a 100-word narrative and submitted it to the *New York Times* for consideration for their "Tiny Loves Stories" column.

Here is that story in its original unedited form.

The Widower and the Washer

"Do you remember what Mom showed you?" I asked my eleven-year-old son.

"The clothes go in there," he answered.

"I know that much. What about the buttons?"

"Change that one to cold."

"And the others?"

"They're good."

"Soap goes in here, right?"

"Yep."

"How much?"

"Fill it to three. Wait. Two."

"Do I have to do anything with the dial?"

"Leave it on normal and hit start."

(One hour later)

"Did Mom ever show you what to do with this error code?"

"Mom didn't get error codes."

"Good thing she left the manual nearby ..."

The *New York Times* did not select this submission for publication, but God had other plans for it. These 100 words were the seed that would ultimately grow into this book, a project which the Lord directed in layers.

After I had collected a handful of personal misadventures with laundry, a conversation with a friend after church one day brought my attention to the opening verses of Paul's letter to the Philippians. It is a passage that speaks about the joy of partnership, or *koinonia* (pronounced koy-no-NEE-ah) as the ancients called it. It was also the passage that Angela and I chose for our wedding ceremony.

From there, it was a matter of telling the story of our marriage while chronicling—in real time—my grief and transition to a new season of life as a widower.

By God's hand, with both wisdom and humor that can only come from Him, laundry was the thing that tied all these serious matters together. It is also the most appropriate theme for both highlighting my struggles and honoring Angela.

As the preceding story reveals, my first attempt to do laundry after my wife's passing was a challenge. After all, it had been thirteen years since I operated a washing machine—since Angela had relieved me of that duty.

Whether she fired me because of my own (lack of) competence, I'll leave for the historians to decide. But one reason for Angela's decision that is *not* subject to debate or speculation is that she genuinely *enjoyed* doing laundry.

It's true. I can back it up with witnesses.

Several years ago, our church held a welcome lunch for new attendees to give them an opportunity to get to know church leaders and their families. We used some icebreaker questions to jump-start conversations, including the standard, "Tell us something unusual about yourself."

Large groups were not Angela's natural habitat, especially if she was expected to speak. But church was a safe space, and these were her people, so when Angela's turn came, she steadied her voice and disclosed that she really enjoyed doing laundry. A voice elsewhere in the room responded, "Oooh! Me, too!" It became quite a bonding moment for Angela and her new friend.

And that is all that I remember about that lunch meeting.

Throughout this book, you will encounter other laundry-related tales, often contrasting Angela's joy and acumen with my own lack of proficiency. At times, the contrast is so extreme that it teeters on absurd. Yet, each story serves as a valuable illustration—a microcosm of a larger truth. Our partnership transcended the division of household chores. It worked into every aspect of our marriage and our shared life.

In the pages ahead, I invite you to join me in celebrating the partnership—the *koinonia*—that Angela and I shared, even as I seek to draw strength from these memories and discern how God might use me in this new season of my life.

The day after we lost Angela, our eleven-year-old son, John Mark, asked, "Who is going to do the laundry?" While this might be an easy question to answer, the mishaps and foibles that follow reveal the wisdom of his inquiry. Yet, like the stories themselves, this question, too, is only an illustration of larger questions.

What will my life look like now?

How do I adjust to losing such a powerful, God-honoring partner?

How will God use me alone after using us in tandem for so long?

I don't purport to know the answers to these questions. When I wrote the first draft of this book, only a few months had passed since I said goodbye to my wife. As you read, you will experience my questions and processing in real time. So, if you're looking for a book that offers you a sure formula for conquering your own grief, this isn't the one.

But if you would like to walk alongside me as we celebrate the thirteen years that I shared with Angela, recall the way that God built and used our partnership from the first day, and turn to the timeless truths of His word as I look ahead, perhaps together we will discover an answer or two along the way.

So join me as I struggle with soap, learn to cope, and proceed with hope.

Part One

The Dynamics of Partnership

I thank my God every time I remember you. In all my prayers for all of you, I always pray with joy because of your partnership in the gospel from the first day until now …
—Philippians 1:3-5

The Great Laundry Takeover

It's not that I can't do laundry. After all, I did my own laundry before meeting Angela, and even now, I have at least a 90 percent error-free completion rate.

Nevertheless, something compelled Angela to take over my laundry after only a couple months of dating. "You know ..." she said with the perfect blend of timidity and optimism. "You can bring your laundry to my apartment and I can wash it there."

The context of Angela's offer and the discussion surrounding it are long lost in the haze of my memory, so I am left to fill in the blanks and theorize (with the benefit of hindsight) what might have prompted her takeover of my laundry. I have a few ideas.

The Clothes

Perhaps the most obvious answer is that Angela saw my clothes day in and day out and decided that something *must* be done. She didn't rush me to the mall to buy a fresh wardrobe, as new girlfriends often do. (We'll go clothes shopping together in Part Four.) Apparently, she was content with my simple jeans and T-shirt style (seasonally accented with a loose flannel or a hoodie as cooler temperatures warranted).

Of course, that was just my casual look. At the time, the dress code at the local bank where I worked required a shirt and tie (with a jacket on standby). On Sundays, I would throw a polo shirt over the T-shirt to achieve whatever level sits between casual and dressy for church.

Staying within the bounds of my "style" (to the extent that the word even applies here), did Angela see something that required her intervention? Were my clothes not clean? Were they wrinkled? (We'll discuss this more in Part Two when we break out the iron.) Did they look like the "other leading brand" pictures from the detergent commercials?

If Angela weighed any of these factors when she took over my laundry, she was too kind to say so.

Still, as I observed her processes, I noted distinct differences. She was selective and specific about what detergent to use. She used the whole dial on the washer, not just the section labeled "normal." And I discovered through Angela that you can store T-shirts on hangers instead of folding them and cramming them into a dresser drawer (or folding them and leaving them *on* the dresser since I'm going to wear them again soon anyway).

Ultimately, I continued to store my T-shirts in a dresser drawer—and still do. But through watching Angela, I determined that you can't fold them fresh out of the dryer. They first have to spend time laid out flat on the bed or the couch before they are eligible for folding. I guess this is the laundry equivalent to letting a roast "rest" after cooking and before slicing.

The condition of my clothes may or may not have been a factor in Angela's takeover. Let's examine another possibility.

The Equipment

An alternate theory involves my washing machine. I vaguely remember some point before the Great Laundry Takeover of 2010 when I showed Angela my own laundry space and equipment (in all likelihood because she asked).

Before we get to the washer itself, I must note that it was in the basement of the small twin that I was living in at the time. You should also know that this house was built in the 1960s in a somewhat swampy town. It was a small concrete space with difficult-to-control dampness issues that would have made any attempt to finish the basement an exercise in futility.

In other words, though it wouldn't be a good setting for a horror movie scene, it was still the sort of basement that a man should not reveal to his date—ever. Nevertheless, Angela was committed, and I trusted her resolve, so into the basement we went, where I could show her my washer in all its glory.

Looking back, it is obvious that my washer was perfectly at home in that small, unadorned, less-than-pleasant basement. Equally obvious, in hindsight, is the fact that Angela must have reached the same conclusion at first glance.

The machine itself was an apartment-scale, stacked washer/dryer combo, hand-me-down unit that my dad acquired for free from a friend who was moving and had no further need for it. So he threw it in the back of his truck and brought it over to my house.

Most of it, anyway.

There were a couple missing panels (and maybe a knob, too). But it wasn't too big for my space or for my needs, and it didn't require a gas hookup, so it was a perfect fit.

More importantly, it ran. The washer did its thing without leaking or spilling, and the dryer worked with reasonable efficiency—although I discovered with the first use that the lint trap was among the missing parts.

(If you're wondering if this machine was even safe to operate, you're asking the right question.)

But did the washer get my clothes clean? Remember those "other leading brand" pictures I mentioned earlier? Over time, my shirts picked up a slight metallic bluish tint (which I discovered once Angela miraculously produced the "after" pictures using her own detergent, washer, and know-how).

Since correlation does not necessarily equal causality, I can't say for sure that my old hand-me-down washer that should have retired to the scrap yard at least two owners ago *caused* the tinted clothes. But a superior explanation has yet to present itself.

Finally, I should note that when Angela and I married and she moved in, we promptly went to the local appliance outlet to purchase a new washer and dryer (to Angela's specifications). I guess she was okay with the basement after all.

The Partnership

Competency and equipment aside, my final theory about what prompted Angela to take over my laundry is that she simply *wanted* to. No doubt, the technical factors revealed to her an area where she could offer me a benefit beyond what I was capable of achieving on my own. Still, she took on the task willfully and joyfully.

Isn't that exactly how partnership is supposed to work: each party acting according to their individual strengths for the mutual and collective benefit of all?

Yes, the Lord was showing us, even as He was preparing us for marriage, how partnership can—and must—be central to a God-honoring, healthy marriage. So in my own desire to act with God-honoring obedience, I gladly handed over free rein of my laundry to Angela. (To be fair, she also spent many years gladly never having to fill her gas tank.)

The ancient Greeks had a special word for partnership. They called it *koinonia*. It is a word that English-speaking Christians have co-opted into our own lexicon through transliteration, though not just because it is chic and cool in America's Christian subculture to throw around spiritual-sounding Greek words. No, we speak of *koinonia* because no single English word captures the depth, richness, and magnitude of the Greek.

We might translate *koinonia* as fellowship, partnership, or communion, but each of those words embodies only one particular facet of the Greek word that means *all* these things—and more—all at once. Fortunately, *koinonia* has rightly earned entry into both the Merriam-Webster and Oxford English dictionaries. So from this point forward, I'll stop rendering it as an italicized foreign-language word.

I learned early on in my years with Angela that koinonia was essential to our success in marriage. Her commitment to full partnership encouraged and facilitated my own participation. Likewise, I am sure the reverse is also true (because Angela often said so).

So let's unpack the first couple of verses from the featured scripture from our wedding ceremony—the Philippians passage that we used to ground and calibrate our marriage—and examine the meaning of this time-tested word.

Koinonia Defined

We're only a few lines into the body of Paul's letter to the Philippians, and already so much jumps off the page. Before we dissect the meaning of koinonia (and at the risk of digressing into a full sermon), let's take a few minutes to meet the people involved in this passage and recap their story.

Paul wrote this letter from prison in response to the generous support the Philippian church provided him. In the first century, prisoners were wholly dependent on outside assistance for their basic needs. They didn't get an allotment of food or prison-issue clothes. If nobody helped them, they didn't eat. Even today, though prison systems provide the bare essentials, anyone who has been on the inside or who has supported friends and family in their incarceration knows how important it is to have commissary money on the books.

So the Philippian church heard about Paul's need, took up a collection, and sent some representatives to visit Paul and deliver their gift.

Paul in Philippi

There is another rich (and beautifully ironic) layer to this story as well. Paul was no stranger to prison. In fact, his first experience with imprisonment came during his visit to Philippi. Acts 16 tells us that upon arrival, Paul encountered a demon-possessed slave girl. Acting on compassion (mixed with frustration—the poor girl was determined to harass Paul), he drove the evil spirit from the girl.

And as the saying goes, no good deed goes unpunished.

Paul soon discovered that the slave girl's owners had been exploiting her turmoil by using her as a fortune teller—and profiting comfortably in the process. With their income stream cut off, they convinced the authorities to have Paul (and his missionary companion, Silas) sent to prison.

Books and movies sometimes portray people not adjusting well to their first night in prison. Paul and Silas also had a hard time assimilating to norms and customs on the inside. As they sat in chains in the darkness, they passed the time singing hymns of praise. We can't be entirely sure what the other prisoners thought of the new guys (who clearly had no idea what to expect) because what happened next was sure to redirect their attention.

While Paul and Silas were worshiping, an earthquake struck and dislodged the doors and chains. The jailer, fearing a mass escape, was prepared to fall on his own sword (which would be a less painful execution than his overseers would mete out). But he stopped when Paul assured him that all the prisoners were still present. Confronted with God's power and grace, the jailer (along with his household) believed and was baptized.

Why does all of this matter? First, it is simply one of the coolest stories in Acts, so it's fun to tell. But more to our point, it helps us understand who the Philippians were and how they related to Paul.

The jailer was likely a retired Roman soldier, with at least enough rank to earn a comfortable assignment in Philippi (a Roman outpost). He was not Jewish and probably had little to no knowledge of Jewish scriptures and customs. Still, he believed and was baptized after he witnessed a powerful display of God's providence.

Also, it is reasonable to imagine that some of the other prisoners believed and were baptized and were also part of the Philippian church. After all, these men all remained when the chains and bars that held them captive were shaken loose. (That—not the earthquake—is the real miracle of that night in Philippi.) What compelled them to stay instead of run? They probably recognized that whatever Paul and Silas had going on, it was worth sticking around to find out how they could experience the same thing.

The Philippian church was more than just a prison ministry, though. Also in Acts 16, before the encounter that would land Paul in prison, he met Lydia, a prosperous member of the merchant class who was worshiping by the river with other women (a common practice in foreign towns that lacked a Jewish synagogue) and whose home was likely large enough to host the newly established church.

Men and women. Merchants and prisoners. Romans, Jews, and foreign converts to Judaism. We can tell from this one short chapter that the church in Philippi was quite a diverse group of believers. Perhaps more than any other church that Paul founded, they were in the best position to relate to him in his present circumstance.

Yet, Paul didn't respond to their gift with an attitude of expectation. He didn't suggest that their gesture was right because it was reparation for his imprisonment in their city. No, he responded with joy. With delight. With sincere gratitude.

Even *before* this gift arrived, that was Paul's attitude toward the Philippians. He thanked God *every time* he remembered them, not just on this one occasion when they showed up with a gift. He prayed for them with joy, not with frustration, fear, or heartbreak.

Why?

Because they were his partners in the gospel—his koinonia. And they had been since the night his chains fell loose so many years before. Their gift was simply an organic expression of their long-standing relationship with Paul.

I mentioned earlier that this word—koinonia—is a rich, multi-faceted word that we cannot represent fully using a single English word. Though there is some variation across translations and between the contextual nuances of different passages, translators use three common English words to represent koinonia; partnership, fellowship, and communion.

To fully understand koinonia, we need (at minimum) all three of these words. Let's take a moment to apply each one.

Partnership

In our lexicon, *partnership* is the word we use to describe business arrangements. In a business partnership, the partners all invest in the enterprise; contribute their time, resources, and talents to the work of the organization; and share in the resulting gains.

In this sense, we understand that our membership in the church and our status as believers is not passive, but participatory. We are partners in the gospel because we all share in some aspect of the work of spreading the gospel and building God's kingdom.

The New Testament describes the church as the Body of Christ because we—as a partnership—are called to do the things that Jesus would do if he were here with us bodily. In fact, when Jesus recruited his first disciples, he called them to work with him—to train as, and become, "fishers of men."

Fellowship

In Christian circles, *fellowship* typically denotes the social aspects of our shared life. This reduction is unfortunate, especially when we consider that our koinonia starts not with our bonds with each other, but with our relationship to the Father, Son, and Spirit. Surely, when John writes, *And our fellowship is with the Father and with his Son, Jesus Christ,* (1 John 1:3) he is not simply inviting us to coffee hour with Jesus.

Likewise, when Paul writes, *May the grace of the Lord Jesus Christ, and the love of God, and the fellowship of the Holy Spirit be with you all.* (2 Corinthians 13:14), he reminds us that our koinonia with God is not something that we put on the calendar; it is a continuous state of being.

The more archaic use of fellowship that still survives in academic circles might nudge us closer to understanding that fellowship is more than an event or activity. It signifies a bond formed in and through a common interest or experience.

Communion

This brings us to our third expression: *communion.* The church generally reserves this word for sacred gatherings (distinct from the social "fellowship" events), particularly the Lord's Supper. This, too, is a reduction. If we look to the secular word, *community*, a linguistic sibling of *communion*, we see how our common bonds take shape. We might call a geographic area a community. Or we might use it as an abstract to speak of hobbies or personal characteristics, such as the "disc golf community" or the "gluten-free community." Regardless of the context, a quick bit of etymology reveals that this word literally means "with unity." It is fitting then, that Christians associate the word communion with the Lord's Supper. In this same gathering, Jesus famously prayed for the unity of his disciples and the church (John 17:20-26).

All of the Above

The Christian koinonia of the church, in its most complete form, embodies everything we call partnership, fellowship, and community—even in the melting pot of the Philippian church with its rich merchants and poor prisoners, Roman soldiers and Jewish converts, and everyone in between.

So what was the thread that bound the Philippian church and Paul in koinonia? The same thread that binds today's church. We are the fellowship of grace because we have all received the free gift of salvation as an act of God's unmerited favor toward us. We are the community whose identity is found only in Jesus, a people defined not by class, ethnicity, or heritage, but by citizenship in God's eternal kingdom.

As Peter reminds us,

Once you were not a people, but now you are the people of God; once you had not received mercy, but now you have received mercy.—1 Peter 2:10

Our identity as God's people is directly related to our status as beneficiaries of His mercy. From this point, we are participants in the work of the gospel, called to be a light in the darkness, carrying the message of God's love and grace to wherever He places us, so that others may experience Him in the work He does through us.

Yet, koinonia is not a concept that suddenly emerged in the first century when Jesus called four fishermen to service. Our koinonia with God and with each other is not just a reflection of the early church, it is inherent in God's original design for creation.

God created the world and everything in it, but He invited Adam to name the animals. God placed His first image-bearers in the garden, but He instructed Adam and Eve (and subsequent generations) to continue this work by filling the Earth with billions more of His image-bearers. God brought forth food from the ground, yet He tasked Adam with taming the land (Genesis 1:28). God paired Adam with Eve because it is good that we should have suitable helpers and that we should not work alone (Genesis 2:18).

Relationship is inherent in God's triune nature, and when He imparted His image on us, He placed in us, too, the capacity and design for relationship. From the very beginning, God established koinonia *with* His people—and *within* His people. And He did it by establishing the most sacred form of koinonia first: the covenant of marriage.

So I thank God every time I remember Angela because she embodied and embraced the koinonia that God built up in us.

The Foundation of Marriage

When I met Angela, I wasn't looking for a girlfriend, for two reasons.

First, I was 36 and had already been married and divorced twice, after which I spent close to four years alone, growing in the Lord and in service to Him. I had largely accepted that God intended to use me as a single man.

Second, despite considering that God may be calling me to remain single, I had recently started dating someone. That relationship turned out to be brief but instrumental in the trajectory of my life.

Several weeks into that relationship, my then-girlfriend invited me to visit her home church on a Sunday morning. We attended the early service at my church then crossed a few ZIP codes to our next stop. When we arrived at her church, a young lady—bundled in a coat, hat, and mittens—waited on the patio to greet us.

That's when I met Angela.

I can't say that she immediately grabbed my attention because someone else had already laid claim to it. In that moment, Angela became one of several new friends that I had made recently through my then-girlfriend.

It was not practical for me to worship with my new friends at that church on Sunday mornings because of my commitment to my own church, but I regularly met up with my new friends at their Friday evening

Bible studies. That lasted a couple of months until my girlfriend at the time and I determined that we were not paired for dating and called it off.

With less sense of obligation, my involvement with the weekly Bible studies became more sporadic, but I kept in touch with several of the guys through social media and made occasional appearances. By the fall, I was participating with more regularity again. Around the same time, Angela—for her own reasons—began to detach from the group. I didn't know her well at that point, but I noticed that the group seemed to lack something in her absence.

One evening, I sent Angela a message on social media, noting that I hadn't seen her around. We had a brief but nice chat where she explained how God was showing her that it was time, for her own growth's sake, to move beyond this particular group. So she explained that she wouldn't be around much for the weekly studies, if at all.

I suggested that since I wouldn't see her on Fridays, perhaps we could meet up for a walk sometime.

I should mention that I still wasn't looking for a girlfriend. At least, I didn't *think* I was. But there was something about the way Angela sought to hear God and walk in obedience that compelled me to pay attention. I was certain that doing so would benefit my own growth.

Our First Non-Date

We set aside some time to meet on Wednesday, September 22, 2010, at Peace Valley Park, which would soon become a prominent place in our story. It would also be the first time that God would show up in a visible, tangible way to give us a glimpse of His hand at work in us.

In our minds, we weren't on a date. We were two friends who wanted to know each others' stories a little better. Still, I came prepared with an extra jacket and an extra bottle of water, just in case I needed to offer a gentlemanly gesture of care and kindness. I soon learned that Angela had rushed to get to the park on time and in her haste forgot to grab a water, so before we even took our first steps, I was 1-for-2.

We walked and talked about all of the things that new friends talk about—background, work, testimony, interests, goals, etc. We reached the south end of the lake and crossed the dam. As we started down the far side, we were discussing future goals. At the time, Angela was a research scientist, but she said she hoped to eventually (insert cleverly worded scientific-sounding phrase that I wish I could recall). I stopped and gave her a puzzled look.

"Wife and mother," she explained.

Despite my mild embarrassment (and her amused smile) at my failure to pick up on her wordplay, something clicked in my head, and I wondered if perhaps this walk was setting *us* on that course. I later learned that Angela had the same epiphany in that moment. We couldn't take our discussion down that path then because something else captured our notice. On the far side of the lake, a massive black storm cloud was approaching with speed and force.

Ripples turned to small waves on the normally still lake. (The place is called Peace Valley for a reason.) Angela retied the red braid of hair resting on her shoulder and we turned and marched back across the dam toward our cars. It was not easy because we were moving directly against the wind and had to keep our heads down to avoid being blown over. (For those of you keeping score, the extra jacket came into play. 2-for-2.) We made it across the dam with sore legs and backs, while the storm encroached on the park.

Then it stopped.

Defying all logic and sense, the massive cloud hung still in the air. We still felt the wind and saw the waves, but by all appearances, the system was being held back. I remembered Jesus commanding a similar storm. *Peace. Be still,* he said with his hand raised. That image stuck in my mind as we returned to our cars, still slowed by the wind.

As soon as we said our goodbyes and were safely in our cars, the storm was on the move again. Buckets of rain fell on us before we had our engines started.

Timing like that doesn't happen by accident. While I left the park that evening fixated on the image of Jesus standing in the boat commanding the wind and waves, Angela was wrestling with a different—but not unrelated—message. *We're going to go through storms together.* That, I later learned, was what the Lord had revealed to her with that scene.

Ratifying the Date

After the profound and enjoyable excursion at Peace Valley, Angela and I were both eager to reconnect. We met up on Saturday for mini golf and ice cream. We didn't call that outing a date either, but that might simply have been because my twelve-year-old son, Kyle, tagged along.

Next, we agreed to meet up again on Wednesday. It turned out that Wednesdays were consistently open on our weekly calendars, so they soon became our standing date night. (But I am getting ahead of myself.) So how should we spend *this* Wednesday? We couldn't replicate the storm vs. hand-of-God episode even if we wanted to. But we still wanted to somehow invite the Lord's presence. So we opted for dinner and a church service (after locating a nearby church with Wednesday evening services).

Dinner was simple. We picked up sandwiches (from Wawa, of course) and staked out a pavilion in a park near the church.

Angela and I both knew that it was time for the "defining the relationship" talk. It was clear to us both that God was building something and that we best not ignore it. I did my best to string together a bunch of sweet words to melt Angela's heart and make her swoon. But I ended up with something corny and more than a little awkward about wanting to start an exciting journey with her.

Angela just leaned forward, propped her chin on her hands, and looked at me with puzzlement.

She must have detected a hint of worry in my face because she smiled and said, "Our journey already started a week ago."

Phew!

I can't recall much about the church service, but suffice to say it was worth our while, and those Wednesday evening services would become a regular feature of our weekly date nights. What I do remember is after the service, as we were driving home, Angela said, "So I guess we can tell people about us?"

I glanced over at her smiling eyes and her red braid and responded with an emphatic, "Of course! I want to show you off," accented by a flourishing wave of my hand.

Then Angela told me that during the church service, the Lord showed her a vision in which I stood at a podium before a large crowd and presented a single daisy for all to see—with the exact same hand flourish. From that revelation on, Angela would be "My Daisy."

Angela and I both understood that we were on a fast track. In the weeks that followed, we did all of the things that new couples do, including meeting each other's families. In short order, we arranged a dinner at her parents' house. But before I could introduce Angela to my family, I lost my father unexpectedly. So Angela's first introduction to my family took place at my father's memorial service.

In addition to Wednesday services and checking all the boxes on our "new relationship" scorecard, Angela and I determined that we should collaborate on multiple spiritual disciplines. Within a couple weeks of our first date, Angela felt the nudge to leave her church and begin attending mine so we could worship together. Actually, "nudge" is not a strong enough word. "Instruction" is more fitting. So I joined her for her final Sunday at New Wineskins, where they prayed over us and sent us off with a blessing.

Angela's first Sunday at my church coincided with Laity Sunday, an annual event in the church's tradition to recognize and celebrate the ministry of the people. Part of the Laity Sunday tradition is that the pastor takes a Sunday off from preaching and hands all duties over to the lay people. As one of the congregation's regular lay preachers, I had the honor of proclaiming the Word that day.

Fitting the occasion, I prepared a sermon from Nehemiah about both God's providence and the people's collaboration to rebuild the walls of Jerusalem in less time (52 days) than it takes present-day builders to get the necessary building permits.

As congregants entered the service, greeters handed each person a LEGO brick. Toward the end of the sermon, I invited everyone to come up and add their bricks to a LEGO foundation sitting on the chancel. If you know anything about modern churches, then you know that not everyone moves with youthful vigor. So our shared reenactment of the rebuilding of the wall took the service into overtime.

The woman sitting next to Angela leaned over and apologized, telling her, "Today is a special day. The service doesn't usually take this long." She had no idea that Angela was the preacher's personal guest.

Also, when we began dating, we stepped away from the Friday evening young adult group. But we didn't want to forgo Bible study, so we continued to use that time slot for our own personal devotions. Angela left the question of what to study completely in my hands.

I chose the book of Philippians for several reasons. First, because it is a generally positive and encouraging book, so it seemed to be a good starting point. Also, because it's a relatively short four chapters, it would be easy to transition to a different book or topic in short order if God showed us a particular area of need.

But Philippians was exactly what He ordered. He was showing us from the start how to partner with Him and build a koinonia together. Months later, when it came time to select a text for our wedding, the choice was clear and obvious to both of us. But I'm getting ahead of myself again (though not by much).

Within a couple months of our first date, I took Angela's dad aside during a visit to tell him I intended to propose to Angela and ask for his blessing. I'm happy to report that I got the green light. What I did not know at the time was while I was rehearsing how to secure a blessing from Angela's father, she was already putting her spare time into perusing rings online.

And by "perusing rings," I mean "finding rings that she liked and sending links to a friend who would not be able to keep the information to herself." So every link that Angela sent to her friend somehow found its way to my inbox. Who could have predicted? Angela—that's who. She didn't like surprises, so she worked to minimize them.

Armed with sufficient data to ensure that it would be impossible to buy the wrong ring, I proceeded to order the one with several small stones arranged in a floral layout. Though it wasn't a typical engagement ring, it was an easy choice, since it reminded me of a daisy. I later learned that around that time, during a Wednesday worship service Angela glanced over at me and the Lord said to her, "When he asks, you can say yes." God also knew that Angela didn't like surprises.

Still, I wanted the right day, the right setting, and the right occasion. Looking at the calendar, I found the perfect day—precisely three months after our first date.

Wednesday the 22nd

At Angela's request, I scheduled a vacation day for Wednesday, December 22, to drive her to an eye doctor appointment. Wednesday was already our standing date night, and with a late-morning appointment, that left the whole afternoon free. Plus, in my corny way of thinking, it wasn't just Wednesday, but *Wednesday the 22nd*, just like our first date. Wouldn't it be a fitting day to level up?

It's okay to roll your eyes. As one friend (the same friend who "spilled" about Angela's ring browsing) once commented on one of our silly Facebook exchanges, "Aww. Nerd likes nerd." Corny doesn't work for everyone, but it worked for us.

My plan was set. After leaving the eye doctor, I suggested to Angela that we go to Peace Valley for a walk, "since we have the time, and it is Wednesday the 22nd." Perhaps I put too much emphasis on the date because in that moment, Angela knew what I had planned. Then again, Angela was smart (and already had some divinely delivered spoilers), so I'm sure she was on to me anyway. The important point, though, is that she was *expecting* my proposal, and *agreed to the trip* to Peace Valley.

December is not warm in this part of the country, so there was already a thin sheet of ice covering the lake. Still, it was a sunny day and more than pleasant enough for a walk. We didn't make it to the dam this time. Instead, we stopped at a small fishing pier. Next to the pier, several hundred birds gathered around a watering hole near the shore.

As we stood on the pier, I broke into a long-winded and poorly rehearsed, rambling lead-up to the big question. For her part, Angela graciously grinned and looked up at me with an expression that said, "I wish you would cut the preamble and just ask already." Which eventually, I did—on one knee, while producing the ring from my pocket.

Angela said yes, I put the ring on her hand, then God did His thing.

The birds broke into a wild cheer.

They didn't chirp, squawk, or do anything that you would expect birds to do. They *cheered*, and they sounded human doing it. Much like the crowd at a sporting event. I will never know if God supplied the birds with human voices for this occasion, much like He did for Balaam's donkey, or if they were a gathering of incognito angels. But one thing we were sure of was that God had plans for our marriage.

From the park, we stopped for lunch, then we visited Angela's parents to share our big news with them. I don't remember much of what was said that day, except that when Angela's mother was briefing me on the ins-and-outs of being a part of the family, she said that "Christmas Eve is always here" (meaning their house).

Level Up

When it came to picking a wedding date, we knew that a long engagement would be silly, but we wanted to give ourselves (and our families and guests) enough time to plan properly. We already had a venue in mind (if you guessed Peace Valley Park, you've been paying attention). But how to pick a date? I suggested that we check to see the next time the 22nd would fall on a Wednesday. It turned out the next one would be June 22, 2011. Six months to the day from our engagement. Perfect.

I'm a man, so I don't remember much of the planning, and not just because most men believe that "weddings plan themselves," but because Angela was highly organized. She kept lists. And it is neither hyperbole nor exaggeration to say that, on occasion, she even had lists of lists. The wedding planning binder was home to at least one such meta-list.

I do remember some people questioning (out loud) why anyone would choose to get married on a Wednesday, with maybe one or two mild grumbles about having to take a day off from work. But we wanted to keep our corny Wednesday the 22nd streak alive, and we knew that in the long run, the mild inconvenience of spending a vacation day wouldn't cause any real harm. Perhaps more importantly, our wedding venue was a public park, so we wanted to reserve a day when we could expect less foot traffic.

Actually, one piece of the planning that I do remember is that when we provided our pastor with our scripture choice, he observed that he had never seen anyone pick that passage for a wedding before. When I later asked him if he saw where we were going with choosing Philippians 1, he responded "partnership in marriage." He saw where we were going.

When it came to picking colors, I had no preference. Angela couldn't decide, so she suggested that we use all of the colors. Remember Roy G. Biv, who taught us the colors of the rainbow in grade school?

He also outfitted our wedding party. Groomsmen in red, orange, and yellow. Bridesmaids in green, blue, and violet.

But you can't have a rainbow without rain.

Angela and I chose an area of the park that had a picnic pavilion large enough to accommodate our guest list and also a large, paved, level patio built into the hillside nearby. We rented a tent and chairs to set up on the patio (with our guests facing the lake), and we used the pavilion for the reception. Yes, it was low-budget, but that was by design. A fancy ceremony is nice, but "fancy" wasn't our style and we preferred to prioritize our resources for long-term plans.

During the ceremony, as our pastor reflected on the message he prepared from Philippians 1, he commented that it was indeed an unusual wedding text. He also said that it was one of the most appropriate choices he had encountered—not only because koinonia partnership is essential to a healthy marriage, but because a marriage rooted in koinonia benefits the church, the community, and the world.

Well, that gave us some high-expectation pressure to live up to. Two nerdy introverts as a beacon to the world? How do we pull that off? Only in hindsight would I remember Angela's vision of the daisy. In the moment, I was too wrapped up in the fact that I was about to exchange vows with a completely wonderful and special woman and that God was building us into an awesome team.

So what sign would He give us that day? Compared to His earlier displays, He showed up with a rather simple moment of confirmation.

There was no rain in the forecast, and the sun had been shining brightly, but as we got to the business of exchanging vows, the rain fell. It lasted into the picture time and yielded the sky back to the sun in time for the reception.

Still, it was enough that Angela and I both knew that God was present in our vows. When people exchange wedding vows, they do so with gravity, and appropriately so. Sickness and health, rich and poor. These are weighty promises that nobody should take lightly. Still, the joy and excitement of the day were enough for us to take our vows with eagerness and anticipation. In that moment, we didn't really think about that sign on our first date, the one that showed us we would go through storms together.

Another part of wedding vows that people tend not to dwell on is the part that says "until death do us part." This is understandable. We say these words thinking about the whole lifetime ahead. Yet every lifetime ends with death. And half of the people who say those words will eventually have to process—and bear the full weight of—their meaning. Sometimes far sooner than expected.

Until Death Do Us Part

"John Mark is safe with your parents. The church is praying, and I'm not leaving. So you don't need to worry about anything. It's all taken care of. Just focus on getting better. I love you."

Those were the last words I spoke to Angela. The final bookend to the millions of words we shared over almost thirteen years of marriage. Unlike the first words of our marriage—vows that we each recited—Angela could add nothing this time because of the oxygen mask over her face.

A Trip to the Emergency Room

Several days earlier, Angela had contracted the flu. From there, she developed pericarditis (fluid around the heart), and her heart was struggling to pump enough oxygen to her brain and other organs.

Now, the mask was not sufficient to raise her oxygen levels, so the doctors determined the only option was to intubate her so they could transport her to a city hospital where they would drain the excess fluid.

At that point, it had been four hours since Angela first called me to take her to the hospital after having passed out. Though she was conscious and coherent, her oxygen level wasn't climbing much, and her heart rate wasn't slowing.

When the doctor took me aside to tell me the plan to intubate Angela, she said, "Your wife is very sick. This is the only safe way to transport her. In her state, I wouldn't be confident taking her into the elevator without help."

Those are scary words, and upon hearing them, it really began to sink in that this was a life-or-death matter. There was a risk, the doctor added, that sedating Angela could stop her heart, so they would be prepared to resuscitate her. But without the procedure, her heart would continue to overwork itself until it could no longer beat. We proceeded with the only option that gave her a chance.

After sending another update to my mother-in-law, I scrolled my conversations until I found a group text with a number of church friends in it and blasted out a prayer request. Responses poured in immediately, and Pastor Jeff made the trip to the hospital to sit and pray with me.

Sitting in a special waiting area off the emergency room (remember—the doctor didn't want to take Angela in the elevator, so they brought everything and everyone to her) was surreal. In my mind, there was no logical outcome other than Angela pulling through. So as I spoke with Jeff, another tab in my mind considered what Angela's recovery would be like over the coming months and what adjustments we would need to make.

Within an hour, a doctor came into the room to let me know that Angela was intubated and on her way to the city hospital where a critical care team was prepared to receive her. He also shared that her heart did stop during sedation, but they were able to resuscitate her.

I felt great relief in that moment. The team's preparation paid off, and the scariest part was behind us. Pastor Jeff went home, and I got on the road for the 45-or-so-minute drive to the city hospital.

It had been raining, and the rain was turning into slush. I called my mother-in-law from the road and updated her. She shared my relief and, like me, concluded that we were through the worst, and it would get better from here. *Angela* would get better from here.

After missing a turn near the hospital in the increasingly miserable winter conditions, I doubled back and found my way into the parking garage. Staffers directed me to the critical care wing, where the doctors informed me that instead of taking Angela to the operating area, they would bring the surgery team to her to drain the fluid around her heart.

They couldn't tell me how long it would take or how soon I could see her. So I sat in the waiting area and finally remembered the snacks I had packed for work eight hours ago but still hadn't eaten. I forwarded the prayer chain email from my church to other praying friends, updated Angela's supervisor, and tried to pass the time reading.

A Sudden Turn

The passage of time across the entire day is hazy, but working backward in hindsight, I estimate it had been over ninety minutes since I spoke with the critical care doctors. When I saw them making their way down the hall to the waiting area, I had the briefest moment of anticipation. But there was something about their gait—the purposefulness and urgency of their steps—that gave me pause.

This is the part where the doctor says, "Your wife has taken a turn ...," I thought.

"Your wife has taken a turn," the doctor began.

I was on my feet and following them back to critical care while the doctor explained that Angela's heart stopped during surgery preparation, and they were able to revive her, but they were worried that they would not succeed if her heart stopped a third time.

The scene when I entered Angela's room was organized chaos. I didn't know what any of the numbers and lines on the screen meant, and I could not interpret the beeps or the technical terms that the doctors shouted to each other.

But there was no way I could misinterpret the doctor administering chest compressions.

I sat resting my head on my palm as I watched. No matter what the staff did, Angela did not respond. Then the noise faded, and the doctor announced the time. 10:25.

The staff pulled me aside and asked if they could call anyone. At that point, I didn't know. All I knew was that I had to call Angela's parents and give them the worst news they'd ever received.

My father-in-law answered, and I told him that Angela was gone. It was the single most difficult thing I have ever had to say to anybody. To hear his grief-stricken reaction made me ache for him even more. I asked if Angela's mother was home, but she had gone to work once she got news that Angela was intubated. So her father was left alone with his grief, with only a sleeping eleven-year-old in the house.

My mother-in-law worked for the same hospital network, but in a different location, so I asked the hospital staff to contact her. After a while, they told me she was on her way.

I called Pastor Jeff, who relayed an update to the church. After a short while, that group text I mentioned earlier chimed. It was Pastor Jeff directing recipients to check their email.

I reached Kyle, and he took the news with quiet shock. I left a message for my sister, then had no more capacity to make additional calls.

By that time, a hospital chaplain was waiting patiently nearby. I returned to Angela's room, which was a stark contrast to the lights, shouts, commotion, and beeps that filled the space moments ago. The room was perfectly still.

Angela was perfectly still.

I stood next to Angela, and the chaplain stepped to my side.

"She was my partner in every way," I told the chaplain without taking my eyes off Angela, knowing this was the last time I would see her.

It was all I could think about. For thirteen years, we had built a shared life—a koinonia in all fullness of meaning. There was not a single aspect of our lives that was left untouched by the other. Now everything about my life would change, and I would have so much to rebuild.

I don't know how much time I spent alone with Angela and my myriad thoughts before I heard a familiar voice coming down the hall saying, "It's not true. It's not true." My mother-in-law came in to the room and collapsed on top of Angela, sobbing. We hugged, we cried, and we were soon joined by some other members of Angela's extended family.

After going through all of the necessary forms with the hospital and arranging for the funeral director to pick up Angela, I worked out some details with my mother-in-law. We agreed that I should be the one to let John Mark know that his mother was gone, but that it would be good for them to be present. So we had a plan for the following morning after everyone got some rest.

Somewhere close to 2 a.m., I began the drive home through sleet-turning-to-snow-making-a-mess. At home, I collapsed on the couch while our dog frantically searched every room multiple times for Angela, whimpering the whole time.

Waking to a New Reality

Though I'm not sure I ever really fell asleep, I woke around 5 a.m. to my phone ringing. I must have sounded asleep when I answered.

"Your message said to call no matter what time it is," my sister Doreen, said.

"I did say that."

"Is everything okay?"

"No. I lost Angela last night."

How could anything—much less *everything*—be okay? Not that I blame the question. I don't (and my sister knows this). It's just that when I considered what was okay vs. not okay, I ended up with a lopsided balance sheet.

Once it was late enough to assume that Angela's supervisor was in the office, I contacted him to share the news with him. Angela's workplace in general—and her department in particular—was a close-knit group that developed genuine friendships. Losing Angela was devastating for them, too.

Texts and calls trickled in—mostly from church members who had received the email the night before.

When I heard my neighbor's skid steer come to life, I got dressed to go out, start up the snow blower, and deal with the overnight accumulation.

The starter cord snapped on the first pull. (Don't worry—it also has an electric start option.)

My neighbor cleared the entrance to my driveway (which had been packed in by the plows) and the main stretch off the road while I dealt with the rest. We were still in the driveway when some friends from church pulled in and hopped out of their truck with shovels in hand. In hindsight, I think they just wanted to check in on me. The snow simply gave them a means of adding some assistance to the visit.

Simple as it was, it was much more help than I was accustomed to after a typical snowfall, and it gave me a sense of how I would have to look at life in this new season. Even though I would have to bear the previously shared weight of managing my house and my life, I wasn't without partners. I still had my koinonia.

Thanks to the added help, the driveway was easily navigable by the time Angela's parents brought John Mark home. Pastor Jeff joined us for this most difficult moment—letting John Mark know that his mother was gone. Even as he processed his initial grief in that moment, when he did speak his questions focused on the practical.

What will we do with the extra car?

Who is going to do the laundry?

As I shared in the introduction, there was something prescient about John Mark's question. "Who will do the laundry?" is a specific way of framing the broader question, "Who can we depend on now that the person we depended on is gone?"

Geography impedes much of my family from assisting with day-to-day needs. Angela's parents are near enough to step in and assist (which I gratefully tell you that they have done and continue to do). Beyond that—for the little things that come up at a moment's notice—the church has our backs. That's where we find our koinonia.

Even as I sat with my son, my in-laws, and my pastor, others in the church were setting up a meal train for us, recruiting people to coordinate a post-funeral luncheon, and writing sympathy cards. This is not to say that only the church responded. Everyone who in some way touched our lives had a response. Angela's office, my coworkers, John Mark's school, friends from our previous churches, and extended family all reached out with compassion, sympathy, and material support.

The next couple of weeks were dizzying as we received a flood of calls, cards, and visits, even while working in conversations with the funeral director and the pastor about Angela's arrangements and memorial service. Most nights, a different family from church would show up with dinner, visit with us, and pray over us. The Sunday following Angela's death, Pastor Jeff shared a special message, speaking to a congregation that grieved as one.

After Angela's funeral, my siblings all came back to my house, and the five of us were gathered in one place for the first time in at least ten years. By that point, nine days had passed, the dog was exhausted from barking at all the strange new visitors, and the flurry of activity finally slowed down.

So many people had said, "If you need anything, just ask." And they meant it. But as I looked ahead and started to think about what moving forward would look like, I wondered.

What do I need?
What do I ask for and what do I do myself?
Who are the best people to ask?

In other words, I began to contemplate what my koinonia would look like and how it would operate in this new season of life.

Part Two

Growing in Our Strengths

… being confident of this, that he who began a good work in you will carry it on to completion until the day of Christ Jesus.
—Philippians 1:6

Man vs. Iron

One of the beautiful things about partnership, particularly the Christian partnership embodied in koinonia, is that the whole is greater than the sum of its parts. Each partner comes equipped and suited for different tasks and roles. This truth affects the makeup of sports teams, business organizations, and church congregations. It applies to marriages as well.

Early in this book, you already determined that Angela was right: I am ill-equipped for any-and-all things laundry related. There is valid merit to your assessment. Still, there is one *particular* aspect of clothing care that draws my domestic weakness into high-resolution focus:

Ironing.

I have an iron. I've even read the manual. Some readers might wonder why anyone needs to read a manual to use an iron. I would agree with you if we were discussing the iron of my youth, with three easy-to-comprehend settings—High, Low, and Off. But I'm not dealing with a basic iron. This is *Angela's* iron.

At a glance, I suspect this iron has more standard features than my car. Dials, a slider, several buttons, and its very own hieroglyphic code. With all these bells and whistles, I'm surprised that I have yet to find a USB port tucked away on it somewhere. But before we analyze the details of Angela's high-powered deluxe iron, let's revisit the iron of my youth so you can see where I'm starting from.

High, Low, and Off. This is easy. This is grokkable. If the iron is on, it's either producing a little heat or a lot of heat. I learned early enough that "a lot of heat" usually means "too much heat," so I operated only on the low setting. This made my job even easier, right? The iron is either on, or it is off. This sounds good in theory, but in practice, I look back and sincerely question the efficacy of my iron (and/or my skills).

A Lesson from History

In my suit-and-tie days working at a local bank, I had a coworker who regularly shared tales from her human resources role at a previous employer. One particularly memorable story stands out. My coworker lamented the times that she would have to coach employees on the basics of life, professionalism, proper dress, and the general expectations of society. "It's frustrating," she told me, "to have to tell your employees to buy an iron *and learn how to use it.*" (Emphasis hers)

Why is this story memorable? Because I heard it so many times—not in the context of meeting icebreakers or presentations, but in one-on-one conversations. I began to wonder if my coworker was trying gently to tell *me* that I should learn how to use my iron. Seriously, her statement was more than just a straight up "buy an iron," comment. Instead, it came across as, "I can tell you have an iron. I can tell that you've turned it on and even put it in contact with your shirt. But I have no idea what happened next." To be fair, I was probably using the iron incorrectly. In those days, I didn't bother with an ironing board. The corner of the bed is firm and flat enough, right?

Soon after that recurring conversation, my coworker retired and the dress code changed, so I didn't think much about ironing or my meager skills in the discipline. Until I saw how Angela approached it.

Of course, she had a proper ironing board, with adjustable height, multiple covers (are they meant to be seasonal, like the tablecloths?), and an attachment at the flat end where one can (in theory) set the iron down so it isn't hanging out on the fabric of the ironing board. She even picked up an over-the-door storage rack to hang the ironing board and iron on the inside of the closet door. I did not know such a contraption existed.

Though my suit-and-tie days of the bank are behind me, I tend, at least in the winter months, to wear button-down dress shirts when working at my part-time library gig. (Remember, my other long-sleeved options are flannels and hoodies.) At least every couple of weeks, Angela would break out the iron and prepare a cycle of my shirts (plus whatever of hers was in the queue) to return to the closet.

Watch and Learn

To my untrained eyes, ironing looked almost ritualistic, and I learned a lot through observation. For example, did you know that the little plastic tabs in the corners of dress shirt collars are removable? I first encountered these little guys hanging out in the dryer (where the lint trap was supposed to be) years ago. It never occurred to me to put them back in the shirts. (A fact that at least one observant coworker must have noticed.)

Back to the ritual of ironing. I remember thinking it odd that Angela would set up in what seemed to be a counter-intuitive space at an odd angle. I also noticed the dog was always agitated during ironing—in part because of the noise generated by the steam, but more likely because her bed was blocked.

In recent months, I've tried in vain to emulate Angela's ritual as best I can recall it. I'm not there yet.

First, with more settings than just High and Low, I had to crack the code of Angela's iron. I discovered that the key is to correctly match the symbols on the dial to words like "cotton" and "blend" on the shirt tag. I would much prefer that the dial include a bright red line with a bold warning that says, "YOUR SHIRT WILL BURN ABOVE THIS LINE," similar to the warnings that ancient people carved into stone pillars to prevent us from building in flood zones.

After decoding the dial, I added water (hey—give me credit for knowing that much), plugged in the iron, and turned the dial to the highest setting my trepidation would allow (the border between "two dots" and "three dots").

A red light came on. By the time I could look up the light in the manual, it had turned green. After briefly considering the possibility of "spicy hot" and "cool mint" indicators, I interpreted the lights to simply mean "stop" and "go"—a conclusion I reached, in part, because I couldn't recall my clothes ever smelling "minty."

So I remembered all about the collar tabs (Angela trained me years ago to remove them when I put shirts in the laundry basket), and I knew to set up at the pointy end of the ironing board.

The Moment of Truth

I started with the sleeves. Did you know that when you smooth out one side of a sleeve, you end up with a big crease on the other side? I must have ironed each side twice before achieving a (barely) passing result.

To deal with my newly created creases, I thought it would be a good time to try the mysterious buttons—the ones with little pictures that resemble the settings on my garden hose nozzle. Steam is what makes an iron work, right? So it was time to take my skill to the next level and do something wet with the iron. I promptly discovered that one button soaked the shirt, and the other button soaked the dog. It seems I didn't know my own strength when it came to handling these buttons.

After another consult with the manual, I managed to make acceptable (not optimum) use of these features. I finished the full cycle of shirts and set the iron on the kitchen counter to cool. (Sorry, I just don't trust that add-on rack thingy.) My conclusion: I need to buy new shirts (which would be its own challenge—see Part Four). Even though I *think* I passed, the whole process was cumbersome, awkward, and clunky.

Still, I had to get through the cooler months with the clothes I had, so I would return several times to the ironing board, trying a different setup each time. After a few weeks, I realized that I was forgetting the first step of Angela's setup: turn on a soccer game.

The benefit of watching the world's most popular sport is that there is always a game happening somewhere around the globe. Even with our very narrow, carefully curated menu of streaming TV services, Angela always managed to find them. The commentary could be in any language, so there was no assurance that we would understand any of it, but background crowd noise (which I learned was an important feature) is linguistically universal. Through this ritual, Angela eventually became a de facto Real Madrid fan.

So, with a soccer game queued up, I was ready to tackle the physical configuration and attempt to optimize my ironing experience. I tried setting up in front of the dog's bed, even though it had moved. I tried different angles relative to the TV. I even tried both sides of the ironing board.

No matter where I set up or where I stood, I felt like a Muppet with an inexperienced puppeteer. That's probably how I looked too—all elbows and bad posture. After repeated failures to discover a workable solution that didn't remind me of visits to the chiropractor, I concluded there was only one possible explanation for my shortcoming: Angela must have somehow, somewhere, found a left-handed iron. I'm certain of it. Try to change my mind.

I'm sure some of you are now guessing that I tried ironing left-handed, also without success. And you would be correct. I am forever doomed to fare about as well with the iron as Angela did with a manual can opener. (All my lefty readers know exactly what I mean.)

But ... I am okay with that. I accept that I simply cannot do everything that Angela did and do it as well as she had. After all, we were designed differently and equipped for different roles and functions, even within the context of a shared life and purpose. That brings us to the next aspect of koinonia that we'll examine.

God Builds and Equips Us

When we run into obstacles and setbacks, it is easy to resign ourselves to defeat. This is especially true when we come face-to-face with our own limitations.

Obstacles and setbacks come in all sizes. Car trouble might be an inconvenience that costs you a little time and money. An illness or a job change might disrupt you for a season. Other changes, like losing a loved one, commence an irrevocable change in direction.

Many of you have seen T-shirts, mugs, or social media posts that declare, "God's not done with you yet." If Paul were writing to the Philippian church today, he might choose similar phrasing. Paul reminds the church (ancient and modern alike) that God still has a purpose and a plan, and He is carrying it out now—despite your inability to see it.

In this way, Paul's words in verse six echo this popular verse from Isaiah (another favorite of sloganeers).

> *But those who hope in the Lord*
> *will renew their strength.*
> *They will soar on wings like eagles;*
> *they will run and not grow weary,*
> *they will walk and not be faint.—Isaiah 40:31*

Whether we are soaring, running, or barely managing to walk, God promises to sustain us and keep us moving forward. Similarly, this verse in Philippians is also about forward movement and the steady, sustained work of the Spirit in the body of Christ.

We sometimes struggle to see this because in modern, Western Christianity we tend to view Jesus' saving work in transactional terms. Come to the altar. Pray the sinner's prayer. Get baptized. Now you're born again. Now you're saved.

But what happens next?

Sadly, many people never consider this question, and too many churches fail to prompt (or anticipate) the question. That was my personal experience. About twelve years passed from the time I received salvation to the time I understood that God wanted me to do something with my salvation.

God's Work in You (Plural)

Paul assures the Philippians that God will carry on the work that He began. This is an imperfect verb in the original Greek, which denotes an ongoing or continual action. Paul doesn't just point out that God started something and He'll eventually finish it. His word choice emphasizes the continuity *between* these two markers.

As an illustration, nobody tunes in to a game to see only the opening pitch and the final out (or the final run in a walk-off scenario). Fans want to see all the plays in between, too.

When things are going well, it's easy to see our forward momentum. But when our momentum changes—as it will throughout life—it's equally easy to feel stuck. No matter where each of us is on our journey, we can look to these words as a reminder that God is still at work in us, even if we don't see or feel Him.

Let's consider the context of Paul's statement. He is not just writing to a single recipient or even to a specific group of individuals. He is writing to the whole community—the koinonia—as a single body. Though it is not obvious to English-speaking readers, the pronoun "you" in verse 6 is in its plural form in the original Greek.

Yes, God saved you—the individual. At the same time, He built you—the koinonia. It is impossible to separate these two concepts. We are designed as relational beings in the image of our relational, triune God. God grafts the individual to the community, and God builds up the community through the individual. Both happen together.

None of us is equipped for all purposes. On the other hand, an assembled koinonia directed by Christ and powered by the Holy Spirit can be fully equipped for all of the purposes that God has established for it.

This doesn't mean that I should bring my wrinkled shirts to church and ask for a volunteer to iron them. (Although I'm sure somebody would. They really are a caring community.) But it does mean that I have a place, even if that place is not at the ironing board. More importantly, it means I have a place with a continuous purpose.

Growing While Serving

As believers, we thrive in community because that is God's design for us. Likewise, the community thrives when its members are growing and serving. These verses reveal that we cannot separate growing from serving. Paul's confidence in the continued growth of the Philippian church is rooted in their partnership in the gospel (verse 5).

The business dynamic of koinonia is on display here. As a body of believers, we are coworkers with God and with each other. Each of us has received the saving grace of forgiveness and the good news of the gospel message. Now all of us contribute to the forward sharing of God's grace as we reveal the Gospel in our actions, our love for one another, and our witness to the world around us.

Years ago, I heard a sermon where the pastor declared that we are not vessels of grace, but *conduits* of grace. The grace that we receive from Jesus is meant to flow through us and beyond us to reach others. We share a continuous flow of grace just as we receive a continuous supply of grace. The work God does *in* us and the work He does *through* us are interrelated and interdependent.

There is one final truth to extract from verse 6 that underscores the point. Twentieth-century scholar and commentator William Barclay points out that Paul chooses some curiously specific words for "began" and "completion," borrowing both words from the ritual of sacrifice.

Just as when I say "opening pitch" and "final out," you understand that I am talking about baseball (without actually saying "baseball"), Paul's Greek-speaking readers would have heard these words with a particular illustration in mind.

In ancient practice, sacrifices (of animals or grain) were symbols of the person who offered them. They were a way of saying, "Here I am, God. I am yours." Jesus, of course, completed the work of the sacrificial system by becoming the final sacrifice, unblemished and wholly sufficient to forgive all our sins. In turn, when we receive Jesus, we accept his sacrifice as our own, saying, "Here I am, God. I am yours."

From this point forward, we belong to Jesus, and through Jesus, we belong to one another in the koinonia that he calls us to. So the continuous work of belonging to Jesus and being conformed in his likeness begins, and it doesn't end until we cross the finish line (or home plate, in a walk-off scenario).

This is especially true in the koinonia of marriage.

Belonging and Sacrifice

Even though marriage is itself a milestone, it is not the end of anything, but the beginning. In marriage, a husband and wife belong to each other, much the same way a believer belongs to Jesus and to others in the koinonia. When you begin a new life together as husband and wife, you change how you operate. You don't isolate from others, but you place some limits on your social and extracurricular engagement. Why? Because you belong to each other, and it is right to establish and protect times and spaces that are uniquely yours.

In every new marriage, the adjustments necessary to make the marriage work (or better yet—thrive) take time, a bit of trial and error, and sacrifice. It won't all be settled on day one. Sometimes an adjustment might be uncomfortable or confusing, with new questions arising every day. Why is there so much stuff in the linen closet? How do I pronounce this word on the grocery list? What happened to my favorite flannel? (I'm sure wives have their own set of common questions, but since I am a man, this is the perspective that I know.)

Coordinating calendars, managing finances, keeping up with the housework, earning money, maintaining spiritual health, making major decisions, and raising children all become joint ventures that take shape based on your individual strengths.

This makes ironing seem like very low stakes, which it is.

Still, how we handle the little stuff informs how we handle the major stuff. If we get hung up on trivial matters, how does that affect the mood at the household Budget Committee meeting? As conduits of grace, it is important that we allow that grace to flow to one another in marriage. Grace allows us to keep the trivial things in perspective, to understand each other's passions and strengths, and to relinquish control of things that are best left in more qualified hands—all at the direction and leading of the Holy Spirit.

When we allow grace to flow freely within our marriages, we inevitably find it flowing *beyond* our marriages. Perhaps a young couple at church will look to you for encouragement. Maybe there is a community need that you as a couple are uniquely suited to address (and mutually passionate about addressing). There is no end to the possibilities that our infinitely clever Creator can work through a koinonia marriage that He continues to build.

Building a Life Together

With the wedding and the honeymoon behind us, Angela and I were—like all newlyweds—eager to start building something—to make our lives into our shared life. We had already established a solid Christ-centered foundation during our dating and engagement months, having forged habits of regular Bible study and daily prayer time together.

While dating, we even learned that my "prayer voice" could soothe Angela to sleep. More than once I encountered silence on the other end of the phone because she had dozed off. (To be fair, her work day started two hours earlier than mine, so she was understandably tired.)

Some Reassembly Required

Having established shared spiritual disciplines, we were ready to tackle the logistics of moving in together. We paid an extra month on Angela's apartment to allow us a buffer so we could move her things into my house in stages. In that time, Angela's first priority was to address the stacks of books that occupied every room in the house. Her solution was to have a bookcase built into the dining room wall. We did, and we moved my books to their new home with little room to spare.

It shouldn't surprise you to learn that Angela bought me a Kindle for our first Christmas as husband and wife. She was determined not to allow the books to reclaim the land. But there's more to combining living spaces than just getting all our stuff in order. We also had to deal with some unexpected pet dynamics.

At the time, I had a dog (Hanna, an exceptionally mellow boxer/shepherd mix) and a cat. They were best friends (except when the cat tried to approach my son Kyle. The dog wouldn't let her near him.) Angela came equipped with her own overly shy cat, Saul, who mostly hid under the furniture.

Saul slowly adjusted to his new living arrangements and housemates. He mostly camped out in the mud room to avoid the other animals. After several weeks, he began to venture out late at night, when I was the only one left awake. As his comfort increased, so did his boldness. He decided one day that he wanted Hanna's bed, so he made himself at home. When the dog wanted to lie down, she tried to nudge him aside, and he would bop her nose. Rather than fight, Hanna whined for me to intervene, and I would have to move the cat.

The situation continued to escalate from there. If Saul found Hanna lying in her bed, he would pick a fight until she relinquished the pillow to him. After a couple weeks of seeing the increasing bullying behavior, Angela and I decided to rehome Saul so he could be in an environment without other pets. Fortunately, squabbling pets were the worst thing we had to deal with in our first summer together.

Functioning as One

With the books and animals settled, Angela and I found it easy to work out all the other little things. Parking, schedules, household chores. Because of our work schedules, Angela did most of the cooking. But since it is something I also enjoy (and—unlike laundry—can execute with proficiency), I took over on weekends.

Angela learned then that when I was in the kitchen, she had the day off. Had she been my culinary arts teacher, she might have checked the "does not play well with others" box on my report card. It's not that I didn't enjoy her company in the kitchen. It's just that I had my own way of doing things that made it difficult for her to jump in and contribute without causing a mishap.

So we spent those early months finding our individual places in our koinonia, deferring to each other's strengths, accommodating each other's needs, and collaborating where we could. God was gracious, and we were grateful that He gave us a relatively stress-free season to get settled in our marriage. Beyond our day-to-day work, we prayed over and planned future decisions, such as when to grow our family and when to buy a bigger house (which we would need before we grew our family).

Our First Storm

Indeed, God had begun a good work in us, and we excitedly anticipated how He might carry on the work He had started, without any thought of where it might end and without much thought of the storms to come along the way. In fact, the only storm we had to face that first summer was Hurricane Irene, which ventured up the east coast in August.

The one nice thing about hurricanes is that they come with advance warning, so we were prepared. That is, we were prepared for a long, busy night with no sleep. Our church at the time served as a short-term evacuation site during local emergencies in our town. I was one of the response team volunteers who, when activated, would arrive at the church to receive evacuees with Christian hospitality.

With the hurricane coming, local officials predicted that a creekside apartment complex would become inaccessible due to flooding and the residents would be temporarily displaced. After Irene made landfall, I received a call around 3 a.m. to get to the church and prepare to receive a couple buses full of residents. Angela was happy to come along and be part of the response.

A normal trip to the church took less than ten minutes. But the same rising creek that prompted the call sat between our house and the church, so we had to go the other direction and take a local highway across the creek, doubling our commute.

Once we were at the church, everyone took care of their respective responsibilities. I dealt primarily with logistics, helping the evacuees find their way in the building, making sure supplies were in order, and keeping in touch with local officials.

Angela, being new to the team, didn't have a role, so she started talking with the guests. Most of them just wanted to be comfortable enough to catch a little sleep, but one person in particular grabbed Angela's attention. While most of our guests nodded off, one young lady remained fearfully awake. She seemed to have nobody with her, so Angela kept her company. She soon learned that this young lady had just moved from California and had never experienced anything like a hurricane.

A quick backstory is helpful here. In the week leading up to Hurricane Irene, our corner of Pennsylvania experienced a minor earthquake—an uncharacteristic event for us. By "minor" earthquake, I mean "some people didn't even feel it" minor. I know this because I was one such person (and yes, I was awake at the time).

The young lady from California confessed to Angela that she laughed when this little quake struck and her coworkers reacted as if the apocalypse was at hand. She was amused because she knew better and her coworkers were scared of nothing.

By contrast, an East Coast hurricane was a completely foreign experience to this California native, and she was scared. Not only was she scared, but she also couldn't understand how her neighbors could just sleep and leave her alone with her fears.

Ironically, a hurricane that reaches Pennsylvania is seldom as powerful as the ones that land in the Carolinas, Florida, the Gulf Coast, or the Caribbean. But that might not have been obvious to a Californian whose understanding of hurricanes came from news reports about Katrina's devastation.

It was Angela who had the blessed opportunity to sit with that young lady while she wrestled with fear, remorse, and whatever else informed her mood in that moment.

I'd like to tell you that Angela's new friend returned to the church the following Sunday and each week after that. But the truth is, we never saw her again. Still, we can't dismiss the seeds that Angela planted that day in the church basement. That was Angela's nature—introverted, not interested in the spotlight, but like a single daisy in the wild, happy to bring a touch of beauty and life to the small space she occupied.

When the roads cleared and Angela and I returned home, we were relieved to find that we had only a minor roof repair to address. It was so minor that it wasn't even worth a call to our insurance company.

Looking Ahead

After fall arrived, Angela and I began discussing major family decisions—namely having children and getting a bigger house. My apartment-sized twin was a fine starter house for the two of us, but we knew we wanted more space before expanding our family. So we established our wish list, geographic boundaries, etc. and perused online listings.

Angela's specifications were more fine-tuned than mine. She had only one childhood home growing up (and her parents still live in that house), followed by less than two years of apartment living before we got married. So she had a specific sense of what the right home would feel like.

Several times in this span of weeks, my work travels routed me past a particular house that caught my eye. It was a ranch-style house with a large kid-and-dog friendly yard mostly surrounded by woods. I liked the setting, and the house itself had similarities to the house Angela grew up in. But I dismissed it because it was in a township and school district beyond our established perimeter.

From the listings, we mapped out a route to do a drive-by of potential houses. Our afternoon excursion eliminated all but one candidate from our list. We returned home and called to book an appointment to see the house that passed the first test. The listing agent informed us that the house was already under contract, but he was still willing to show it. We didn't want to take the chance of seeing the house, wanting the house, and being told we couldn't buy the house, so we passed.

We returned to the online listings and started a township-by-township search to find more candidates. The top result on our first search was the house that I had seen—and dismissed—during my work travels. The municipal boundary was about a mile from where I thought it was. Angela and I agreed it was worth taking a closer look, so we booked a showing.

We had two concerns. One, we noticed that the house had been listed for close to a year. Two, the seller had substantially reduced the price in the summer. Despite our questions, we set up an appointment for early January.

Jesus in the Storm

When we arrived, Angela quickly picked up similarities to her parents' house, which gave her an instant sense of comfort. The seller had mostly moved out, so the house was sparsely furnished. The back bedroom was completely empty, but the contents of the middle bedroom grabbed my attention.

A single end table sat in the corner of the room. On top of the end table stood a foot-tall statue of Jesus. His feet were surrounded by waves, and his arm was outstretched, palm out. The words "Peace. Be still." were inscribed on the base of the figure.

"This is our house." I said to Angela and pointed to the statue.

She nodded, and we finished the tour, making sure to get answers to our questions. We learned that the sizable parcel (close to eight acres) came with a hefty tax liability that turned off many potential buyers. And the late summer price drop? That was a gift from our old friend Irene, the hurricane we met earlier. The house previously had a partially finished basement rec room, but enough water came in during the hurricane to force the seller to strip the basement to the block.

These items were not deal breakers for us, so after some deliberating and prayer, Angela and I were certain we had found the right house—she because of the similarities to her childhood home, and I because of the statue of Jesus reminding us how we started this journey together. So we submitted a fair offer to purchase the house.

And we were rejected.

A Step of Faith

Our Realtor told us that the seller was comfortable with the price we offered (which was a shade lower than the listing price), but she was not willing to accept our contingency clause. Upon our Realtor's advice, we conditioned our offer on the successful sale of our little twin, which we had recently listed. We weren't interested in being landlords, and we were sure that managing two mortgages would put too much strain on our finances.

This was early 2012, and the housing market was still feeling the ripple effects of the 2008 collapse. If we removed the contingency clause from our offer, we would be taking a huge risk. But after more prayer and deliberation, that's what we did. We reasoned that God led us to this house, and He confirmed this to each of us in our own way, so He would surely find us a buyer for the twin in due time.

The seller accepted our revised offer, and we had our sights on a settlement date about two months out. So Angela and I decided to implement the next phase of our long-term plan. Before January was over, we confirmed that we would be new homeowners *and* new parents before the end of the year.

It was an exciting time, but not without its hiccups. Somewhere in the chaos of packing up our house, the cat got scared enough to take off out an open door. Over the next few weeks, we and our friends would stop by, cat carrier in hand, to try to find her and bring her home. We spotted her a couple of times, but she never let us get close enough to retrieve her.

Meanwhile, at our new home, we were getting settled and organized. The middle bedroom would be our temporary storage area for the unpacking months, but we only had six months to go before it would be repainted and outfitted with a crib. The year was a blur, and our first cycle of seasons revealed that new windows and central air would top our home improvement wish list. We assumed we would take care of these things as soon as the twin sold.

After several months with no activity on our house for sale, we shaved a bit off the price. We had a few showings, but no offers. Still, it was the most affordable house in the ZIP code—a perfect starter place for first-time home buyers, so we were confident it would sell any day now.

Until the market changed.

By that time, 2008 had fully caught up to us, and several larger properties in the town had been foreclosed and re-listed. These houses were 50 percent larger than ours, but selling for the same price. We didn't entertain a single showing after that.

So as the old house chiseled away our savings month after month, and with the birth of our son fast approaching, we learned that Angela and I had different thresholds for financial security. Angela was used to a big cushion in the bank, while I figured that as long as the paychecks kept coming, we were fine. Years later, I would hear Dave Ramsey talk about, "your wife feeling anxious in a place you don't even have," and nod with familiar understanding.

Still, we were sure that God had led us to this house and blessed our purchase. We trusted that He was up to something. We just had no idea what it could be.

God's Timing

It wasn't until the following February, months after our son was born (don't worry—we'll backtrack and give you a proper introduction) and a full year after we had listed the twin that we received an answer.

By this point, I discovered that I was actually equipped with one of those anxiety zones, too. Mine was just harder to find than Angela's. Our savings had dropped to where we could manage one more mortgage payment on our extra house before we had to figure something out. I should note that both of our mortgages were with the same bank that had supplied my paycheck for more than a decade. So default would not only put our houses at risk, but my employment as well.

It was here that we began to learn that God's timing is often perfectly calibrated to reveal that the solution is His and not anybody else's.

Out of the blue, I got a call from a friend I don't hear from often. After our perfunctory catching-up, he asked if I still had the house on Clymer Avenue. I told him I did, and he asked if I would consider renting it. Of course, I was happy to hear what he had in mind.

He explained some friends of his had been sharing a house with extended family, but because of a change in circumstances, they needed to move into their own place and couldn't afford market rates. But they *could* afford what we needed to cover payments on the twin.

By the end of the month, we had a lease in place that worked for everyone, and they were moved in.

God had a plan for our house situation the whole time, but His plan wasn't about us. Yet, He used us to play a role in His plan, and for that we were grateful, though if we had authored the plan ourselves, we would have written it differently. But I've learned over and over that the plan God gives us is seldom the one we would choose for ourselves.

When Life Forces a Rebuild

In the same way that my old twin house was suddenly too small when Angela and I married, our house suddenly seemed too big without her to share it. It's not that we had unused space. At roughly 1,300 square feet, our house is small by modern standards. Still, we had spent the past twelve years growing and settling into the space we had, while slowly accumulating a basement full of stored items as we continuously made room for present-day needs in our main living space.

Even while I was still wrestling with my deepest grief, I experienced the conflict of the choices I had to make. Part of me wanted to leave things just the way Angela liked them in some hope of feeling her lingering presence. But another part of me recognized that doing so would eventually conflict with what was practical, so I would need to make at least some changes.

Still another part of me wanted to sweep through the house and change *everything*. My intent was not to purge, but to exercise some measure of control over my life, which had been thrust into chaos and upheaval.

But I wasn't in control. If I were writing the script for how my year would play out, I would have written it very differently. Angela would be alive, not only for 2024 but for many years beyond, and you would not be reading this book.

But it was God's purview to begin His good work in us *and* to see it to completion. For reasons I don't know, Angela's work in this life had reached its conclusion, while my work continues without her.

That's how I had to look at my life (and how I *still* have to look at it). God was beginning a new work *in* me—and a new work *for* me (which begins with this book). But He began this work not as an abandonment of the work He did in and through our marriage, but in a way that builds on all that Angela and I shared in our koinonia.

I knew that eventually I would need to make some major decisions about the house and similar financially significant matters, but by God's grace, He set me in a place where I didn't need to make any hasty decisions. I would have a little time—maybe a couple of years—to pray and assess where He was leading me.

Sorting through Memories

So what did the beginning of this new season look like for me? After cleaning out obvious things like open food packages that had printed expiration dates, I decided to start with the easiest section: the basement.

One area of the basement had been reserved for things I determined we no longer needed but were waiting for Angela's approval before final disposal. This could be anything from unneeded furniture to toys our son had outgrown to appliances that had stopped working, plus a shelf full of smaller books, toys, and miscellaneous household goods.

It was an easy decision to haul all the broken appliances to the recycling center and donate the usable toys and household items.

I'm glad I started by getting those items out of the way. When I began opening bins with more recent items, I slowed down—partly because of the weight and enormity of the task. But more so, it was because I discovered all the things Angela had saved. I found several bins full of her childhood memories, school work, college papers, and other mementos she had accumulated long before we ever met.

Those bins would take more deliberation and time. I had no personal memory to associate with any of the items inside of them, but they were still things that shaped Angela's mind and personality over the years.

As I opened those bins, it occurred to me that someone will eventually go through all the things *I've* set aside and wonder what significance these items have. So I changed course and sorted through my own stored belongings, and I got rid of much of it. Things that Angela and I had recently accumulated together largely met the same fate. Anything I no longer needed and had no sentimental value went either to the trash or the thrift store as determined by condition.

Even that was a slow process. I could do only so much at once before it weighed on my mind. I might not have been tearing down all that Angela and I had built, but I was, in a way, parting with past seasons of our shared life. Of course, I still saved some things even if they didn't have immediate practical value. We still had plenty of John Mark's old toys, so I consolidated them into age-appropriate bins, which forced me to limit how much I kept.

I figured that way, if we had guests with small children, I could bring up the right bin(s) of toys for them to use. Plus, I still have a little something on hand for when (if) the time arrives that I need to entertain grandchildren.

Cleaning out the garage came next, and that was relatively simple considering it is space that was almost exclusively mine. In fact, I probably would have started there had the weather been warmer. Making changes in our everyday living spaces would prove much more daunting. And as of the first draft of this writing (nine months since Angela's departure), most of that remains undone.

So far, the biggest change I've made is in the spare bedroom, which doubles as office and recreation space. But even that reshuffle is more about optimizing my writing space and accommodating John Mark's changing needs and interests as he enters middle school. It's a change that probably would have happened even if Angela were still here. When I "took over" the spare room in 2020, Angela essentially conceded the territory, declaring that she "didn't understand" how I had the desk arranged.

Knowing My Limits

Eventually, I would need to tackle the things that were undoubtedly ours or hers. Slowly, I've been moving things out of the linen closet, the bathroom closet, and similar spaces. I might top off a bag on trash day because that's all that I can handle emotionally. Or I'd leave a bag of books in the library donation bin. (Yes, Angela had a few books—but mostly these were mine.)

Someday I'll have to deal with the bedroom. We'll talk about emptying the closet and donating clothes in Part Six. That still leaves the dresser and other items to deal with, and I'm not there yet. Which is not to say I am stubbornly leaving things unchanged, just that this is the weightiest part of the process.

For example, Angela always slept with a fan blowing because she needed the noise. I prefer not to have the fan on. So I've not turned Angela's fan on since February 11, 2024. But as of this draft, I haven't moved it from its place on her nightstand either. Someday, I will. When I do, it will probably be in the context of fully rearranging the room. But today is not that day.

I think the reason moving the bedroom around is at the bottom of my list is twofold. First is the obvious reason—it is the most emotionally heavy change. It produces the biggest reminder that Angela has departed from this life, and our reunion does not come until the next life. But there is a second reason. Rearranging the bedroom affects me—and only me.

Every other thing I touch prompts a question— how does this affect others? The reason Angela was so reluctant to throw things away (even broken appliances) was because she thought they *might* be useful someday. So that's the filter through which I run these decisions. If this item is no longer useful to me, where *can* it be useful? Having thrift stores, libraries, and similar places to donate things is certainly a start.

But what about more specialized things? I knew I had to get all of Angela's art supplies into the hands of an artist who would make good use of them. We already discussed curating toys for guests and future users.

So piece by piece, I let go of things. Of stuff. Not memories, just the objects.

This reshapes my thinking going forward. As more years progress, will I be inclined to accumulate less? Quicker to give away things I no longer need? I like to think so because eventually, someone will need to clean up after me. It is my hope that when I am gone, what I leave behind matters and that my legacy is worth passing on—just as Angela's legacy continues through the possessions I can share and—more importantly—through the story I am privileged to preserve with this book.

Part Three

Growing in Teamwork

*It is right for me to feel this way about all
of you, since I have you in my heart and,
whether I am in chains or defending and
confirming the gospel, all of you share in
God's grace with me. God can testify how I
long for all of you with the affection
of Christ Jesus.*
—Philippians 1:7-8

Nobody Can Fold Sheets Alone

For as much as Angela kept me away from the laundry (for her own sanity's sake), she allowed me limited opportunities to participate—in controlled situations. Specifically, she let me help her fold the sheets. Okay, it's more accurate to say she requested my help. And having teamed with her on this task, I've concluded that it is an endeavor that even the most adept among us dare not try alone.

That's part of being an expert, right? Knowing when you need help. Knowing when a task requires more than one person.

Some of us are slow to grasp this concept. That is why when you buy new assemble-at-home furniture, you see **TEAM LIFT** in big bold letters on the side of the box, accompanied by a picture of two stick figures lifting a box (bending at the knees—not the back). So whether you read English or hieroglyphics, you are appropriately warned that you cannot lift this box—which, incidentally, surpasses the human arm span—alone.

Angela, being the expert in both laundry and assessing spatial relations, knew the sheets exceeded her arm span, so she recruited my help. My job was to follow her instructions to the letter, and everything would work out. Easy, right? You would think so. But I *am* a member of the sex that needs pictographic reminders of the minimum number of stick figures required to lift a big box. So, like the assemble-at-home furniture, Angela used as few words as possible in her instructions, relying instead on visual cues.

The Dance

First, Angela would hand me my corners, and we'd step back from each other carefully. She would take a step, and I would follow—she the choreographer and I the student. Quick aside—I don't dance. Ironing isn't the only context where I move with the grace of a Muppet. Now that you have a mental image of an awkward guy and his all-too-patient wife stretching out a sheet between them, you're all caught up.

Step one, it turns out, was easy. Angela would look at me with her serious I'm-the-teacher-now-do-as-I-do look, bring her hands together, and nod toward me. As one, we would each bring left and right together. She'd gently shake the sheet, and I would join her. And just like that, the first fold was complete.

She'd queue up that we're-doing-the-next-step look, let go of the joined corners with one hand, reach for the newly created corner at the fold, and bring it level. I'd watch and mimic, and together we would bring the sheet up ...

Twisted.

Now, I would like to blame this mishap on the fact that Angela was left handed and I am not. But shouldn't that make folding a sheet easier? After all, if her dominant hand is across from mine, they can team up and work together. Well, I tend to see radial symmetry before I see mirror symmetry. So when Angela reached for the new corner with her right hand, I did the same with my right hand.

Twisted.

Followed by Angela's let's-try-that-step-again look.

So try again we did and—with some careful and intentional observation—we'd complete the second fold. Now with a long, narrow four-ply sheet between us, we had to fold it in half at the equator. This is still a two-person task because the sheet is playing The Floor is Lava (even though we are safe standing on it).

So we'd walk the two ends together, lifting as we did to keep the sheet out of harm's way. Then Angela had a choice to make. Should she hand her end to me and retrieve the loose end, or should she hold while I retrieve? In her wisdom, Angela assigned me the simpler task—stand still and hold the sheet—while she completed the part that required movement. I'd like to tell you that this worked every time and we never dropped the sheet. But ... this is a Christian book, so such dishonesty wouldn't be appropriate.

Still, let's assume I got my part right (which, eventually, I did), and we could move on to step four. Step four was the easiest step for me. All I had to do was hold the sheet while Angela completed another lateral fold and graciously took the sheet from my hands. My task was complete. Or so I thought. Up next, we had to start this whole dance over again with the fitted sheet.

Where Science and Art Collide

Much comedy has already been written about fitted sheets and the impossibility of folding them, so I won't rehash others' jokes here. Besides, those jokes wouldn't apply because Angela somehow came up with *corners* on these things so we could fold them just like a regular sheet. Corners! On a fitted sheet! Where did she find them?

Yes, Angela was good with spatial relations, but finding corners on a fitted sheet must be the result of either expert origami or advanced physics (involving access to higher dimensions). Whether she was using art, science, or both, it's outside my skill set. I have not tried to replicate her work.

But I *have* tried folding sheets alone. More on that in a moment.

I could ask my son to help. After all, he knows my challenges with laundry. Remember, this is the kid whose most helpful words of wisdom in my moment of struggle were, "Mom didn't get error codes." But since he knows about this project, he'd probably respond to a request to fold sheets with his signature deadpan look and say, "You need this for your book, don't you?"

If I ever print a second edition, I might try this. For now, I'll try folding the sheets myself. My first challenge is the whole arm-span limitation. Fortunately, a sheet is more malleable than a tightly boxed furniture kit. So if I can ignore the arm-span challenges at the home improvement store, I can do it here, right?

Trying to Do the Task Alone

Well, not really. I might be able to stretch wide enough horizontally, but my arms are neither long enough nor numerous enough to pick up all four corners. I already know that laying the sheet out across the floor and folding it there is not an option, at least not if I want to have clean, dog-hair-free sheets. If I had a clothesline in my backyard, I could complete some folds on the line until the arm-span issue would be moot, but that is not an option right now either.

I found I could lay the sheet out across the bed and fold it there. With this method, I lined up the corners on the first fold after about ten moves and a whole lot of back and forth walking around the bed. So far so good.

Until I tried to complete the second fold. Then the corners from the first fold didn't want to stay in alignment.

Long after I stopped counting movements, I resigned myself to the reality that "close enough" will have to be good enough. So my sheets are now tucked, imperfectly, in the linen closet, with corners protruding at odd angles—except for the fitted sheets, which have no corners, just imperfections.

I remembered all too late the shortcut to this whole mess that I used to use in my bachelor days, which is to wash the sheets, then immediately put them back on the bed. Genius! No folding necessary—ever. Then the spare sheets could remain in the linen closet, folded neatly with corners perfectly aligned (even the fitted sheets!), right where Angela left them.

But it is too late for that. Instead, every time I open the closet, I get to see my inadequate, solo rendition of the folded sheets and sigh with a fresh reminder of how much I miss Angela. How much I long for her to still be present with me. Not unlike how Paul longed for his partners in the Philippian church.

Sharing in God's Grace

Paul's longing for the Philippian church is obvious; he states it outright. There's not much left for us to interpret in verses 7 and 8, but we should still consider where his longing comes from and why.

Does Paul miss the Philippians? Clearly. But is this simply because he likes to be around them or is Paul's longing rooted in something more? Like, perhaps, his appreciation of their work for Christ's kingdom. Or maybe the circumstances of Paul's imprisonment amplify his longing.

If this were a multiple choice test, I'd answer D) All of the above.

In previous verses, Paul laid bare his love for the Philippian church and the joy that flowed naturally from his relationship with them. As Paul expounds on his joyous reflection, he makes note of his circumstances, yet Paul's imprisonment does not diminish his joy.

He expresses no envy or resentment toward his koinonia, even though they are free and he is not. In fact, he does the opposite; he points out that it doesn't matter. Why? Because their separation and their disparate circumstances do not change the fundamental reality of their koinonia.

What We Do or Who We Are?

In verse 7, Paul says—chains or no chains—that the Philippian church *shares* in God's grace. Most English translations treat the syntax of this verse a little differently. They render this phrase as *partakers in God's grace,* using the noun form in reference to the Philippian church rather than the verb form as shown above in the New International Version.

Although the reader takes the same general meaning in either translation, treating this word as a noun is more beneficial, and not simply because it more accurately reflects the Greek. The distinction is that Paul isn't just commenting on what the Philippians do, but on *who they are*.

Being the church isn't just their work or their good service. Being the church is a substantial part of their identity. The same holds true for us in the twenty-first century church. Of course, Jesus establishes our identity in him through the saving grace of his death and resurrection. But our Christian identity is fully *expressed* in koinonia with other believers.

If we examine the original language, the English word "partaker" is translated from the Greek word *soongkoinonos*. Nested in this word is the same root from which we derive koinonia, but with a prefix added.

Let's break it down:

Koinonia = partnership, which derives from *koinonos* (partner). Add the prefix, and we end up with *soongkoinonos*, meaning "partaker *with*."

This adds a layer to Paul's relationship with the Philippians beyond just "coworkers." They are more than a group of people who simply do stuff together. They are united first by a common source—a shared identity.

As English speakers, we generally use the word "partake" when we receive something together, not simply when we are doing things together. Many of you probably thought of your communion liturgies when you saw the word "partake" above. If so, then you get a sense of what Paul is saying.

The Philippians are Paul's partners in the work of the gospel (sharing the good news) because they were first partakers in the singular transforming grace of forgiveness and restoration through Jesus' death and resurrection. They didn't just do things in common. They were all made into something in common.

The Value of Connection

The common grace that the entire church across the world and throughout history shares is a recurring theme in Paul's letters. In Romans 11, Paul describes the grafted branch (the gentile believers) as sharing in the root of the tree. Although the root (Israel) and the grafted branches previously came from separate sources, God's work of uniting them in Christ established a single, shared identity from the point of salvation forward.

Elsewhere in his writings, (Romans 12, 1 Corinthians 12, Ephesians 4) Paul talks about the distribution of spiritual gifts among believers. He describes the separate gifts given *by the same Spirit* (1 Corinthians 12:4), resulting in a church—a koinonia—whose *many parts function as a single body* (1 Corinthians 12:12). Our shared work for the gospel is a natural result that flows from our shared identity.

Neither Paul's chains nor his separation from the Philippians undo their koinonia. Of course, as twenty-first-century readers, this is an easy notion for us to grasp. Thanks to modern technology, someone living in Toledo can work in Tokyo just as easily as if he were present at his employer's office half a world away.

While Paul's letters were slower than modern communication systems, they were every bit as powerful, connecting congregations across the entire geographic reach of the church. They still connect us all today, to both the ancient church and to one another. Knowing that their connection transcends geography, Paul joyously celebrates and encourages the work of the Philippian church, even though he would prefer to be present with them.

In this way, the longing that Paul describes is unique to this particular church. In fact, Paul has a contrasting analysis of his geographic separation from some other churches. To the Corinthians, he suggests that because of his frustration with them, his temporary absence is good for them in that season (2 Corinthians 13:10). That is not to say that he loves them any less, but that God's kingdom purposes are better served by their physical separation.

The Depth of Longing

As for the Philippians, Paul longs for them with *affection*, which might not be a strong enough word to convey Paul's complete meaning. In fact, the King James version says that Paul longs for them *in the bowels of Christ*.

I find this literal rendering of the original Greek fascinating. It reveals something about how people in the first century understood the ways that we experience different sentiments. In our culture, we speak of the heart (feelings) and the head (thoughts)—and not much else.

For the ancients, attitudes and thoughts were all more or less wrapped up in one bundle in the heart. But certain feelings, particularly the strong ones that *demanded a response*, resided in the gut. In the bowel.

Whether we read a translation that says, *Jesus had compassion ...* or *Jesus was filled with bowels of mercy ...* (Matthew 14:14, for example), we see that what happens next is Jesus *does something* about it. His compassion compels him to address whatever pressing need informs his sentiment. With this insight, we get a sense of the deep longing that Paul conveys—a longing that Paul surely understood might never be satisfied.

When I consider how deeply I miss Angela, not just because of our mutual affection, but because of our partnership, I feel that longing in some uncomfortable places. And I do so especially aware of the proximity problem that Paul faced.

I am bound to this life, chained to a mortal body subject to fatigue and deterioration, surrounded by a world where sin and decay reign. Angela, on the other hand, knows only freedom now, having completed the race and entered into victory.

But like Paul, my longing isn't the end of the story. He was just getting started at this point in his letter, and God still has more work for me to complete—work that is not separate from my koinonia with Angela, but that flows from what He spent the past thirteen years building in us.

A New Addition and New Challenges

In the koinonia of marriage, no area reveals the need for partnership and teamwork more clearly than parenting.

Angela and I welcomed John Mark into our family in October 2012. We were grateful that Angela's pregnancy and delivery were free from complications. And we were especially grateful that the Lord engineered the perfect timing for our son's arrival.

John Mark was due the last week of October. Early in the month, with just a few weeks to go, we were arranging the final details. His room was ready, and we had assembled all of the basic supplies. Family members were on standby—especially Angela's parents, who were eager to welcome their first grandchild. Even my assistant at the office was using up some vacation time so she could be recharged and ready to cover for me when I had to take a few days off.

Working Around the Storm

On a Monday afternoon in early October, Angela arrived at her OB-GYN's office for a routine appointment. She checked in and took a seat in the waiting room. A moment later, she returned to the reception window and said, "I think my water just broke." The staff quickly got her to an exam room, and she called me.

I should note that if Angela could have scripted the circumstances of her labor and delivery, she would have come up with something very similar. She was already in the doctor's office—a clean, properly equipped environment with the right experts present. This scene is further evidence that God knows us better than we know ourselves.

I picked up Angela and drove her up the road (less than half a mile) to the hospital. Her labor went well into the night, and I fought to stay awake for her sake. This became more difficult after the West Coast games ended, leaving nothing worth watching on TV. From there it was a contest to see if John Mark could beat the sunrise to the horizon. He did—but not by much.

After John Mark was born, we had only a couple weeks of getting settled with our tiny (under six pounds) addition and his ever-observant ice-blue eyes before our lives were disrupted by another storm—Hurricane Sandy, which would soon become known as Superstorm Sandy.

As hurricanes go, Sandy was weird. This late-season hurricane made landfall on the mid-Atlantic coast, farther north than most hurricanes. It was also accompanied by an unusually early frost. As a result, Sandy became a combination hurricane-plus-ice-storm—all before the trees had shed their leaves.

If you think this is a recipe for a huge mess, you're tracking with me. Power outages were widespread, and our house was without power for over a week. With only about a dozen homes serviced by our spot on the grid, we were near the end of the restoration queue. So we lived temporarily in a friend's spare bedroom, with John Mark sleeping in a laundry-basket-turned-bassinet.

Still, we were thankful. We were grateful for our friends and their hospitality, and for the fact that had John Mark not arrived early, we would have had significant difficulty getting to the hospital *during* the hurricane and its aftermath.

Leaning on Our Gifts

Like all new parents, Angela and I wondered how our son's personality would develop. What would interest him? In what areas would he discover talent? Most importantly, how would God use him?

Early on, we noticed his tendency to fixate on seemingly empty spaces. To me, it looked as if he was seeing things that I couldn't see. I even wondered out loud that he might be seeing angels. One of Angela's gifts was that God sometimes gave her glimpses into the spiritual world, so I didn't have to speculate. She saw what our son saw.

Of course, not all spiritual beings are friendly. On one occasion, when John Mark was still small enough to tote in a carrier, we were out at a family function, and our son began wailing. There was fear on his young face as he fixated on the corner of the room. Our attempts to soothe him were fruitless. Finally, Angela suggested we should leave. (It was late enough that doing so was not awkward.) In the car, she confirmed what I suspected. A hostile spiritual being—a demon—was present and harassing John Mark.

As parents, we wanted our son to grow up with a good grounding in the truth of God's word. We made the decision to keep him with us during worship services instead of taking him to the church nursery. This often meant holding his carrier in both hands and gently swinging him to keep him calm during the sermon. It was certainly a trying upper-body workout, but for the most part, it worked.

From his earliest days, John Mark grew up understanding that being in worship together was normal. As he learned to walk, he would interact more with the service. He'd come up front and dance during the music. Then at home, he would gather some stuffed animals together, get out his toy drums and "play" our worship songs for his own little plush congregation.

Angela and I also wanted to be sure that John Mark understood that Jesus is a part of *all* aspects of life, and not just someone we visit and talk about at church. From his first day, we prayed together at night, and we read daily Bible stories together.

We started John Mark off with an illustrated children's Bible that he was happy to read through over and over. It brought us great delight to see how the stories would become familiar to him and that he would occasionally "read" to us when he was old enough to recount the stories on his own.

As happy as we were to see our son growing in his knowledge of the Bible, it was not without its challenges. On one memorable occasion, I had a rare Saturday to sleep in, but my rest was cut short when Angela came into the bedroom and told me that she needed me to deal with something.

Startled, I expected to find someone injured, something broken, or both. It was nothing of the sort. The emergency, it turns out, was exegetical. This was my area of gifting—not Angela's.

She brought me up to speed: John Mark had been carelessly jumping on the couch despite Angela's repeated instructions to stop. At one point, he slipped and bumped the table, and it hurt. Angela wanted him to see the connection between his actions and the outcome, so she asked him why he got hurt. John Mark was just barely old enough to start talking, and he said, "God did it."

"No," Angela answered him, "God didn't do that. He's loving, and He doesn't hurt us."

To make his case, John Mark marched to his room, grabbed his children's Bible, opened to the story of the ten plagues, held the passage up to his mother, and pointed to a picture of people bandaging their sores.

That's when Angela handed the discussion off to me.

Because her gifts were different from mine, she discerned that I was better equipped to explain how the ten plagues fit not only into the Exodus narrative but prepared the world for an even greater redemption and rescue that would ultimately come through Jesus' death and resurrection.

Still ... how does anybody explain that to a two-year-old?

While we didn't let John Mark skip kindergarten and proceed straight to seminary, we enjoyed seeing God's Word taking root and watching our son's spiritual gifts emerge. Apart from his intelligence and capacity to accumulate knowledge, John Mark continued to have occasional glances into the spiritual world for a while.

One day, he was playing in his room and came out to tell us there was a dragon outside the window. It would be easy for parents to chalk this statement up to a vivid imagination amplified by play time. But Angela was familiar with visual manifestations of the spiritual realm and the forms that demons commonly use, so she decided to see for herself. Sure enough, she confirmed the presence of a hostile spirit, and as a family we prayed together until it fled.

On another occasion, John Mark came out of his room after bedtime to tell us that the butterflies were keeping him awake. We tried to encourage him and assure him that these were angels—friendly spirits—and that they wouldn't harm him. Nevertheless, he found them too distracting and asked not to see them.

Since that time, God has quieted this gift in our son. Perhaps He will someday restore it, and John Mark will once again get glimpses into the spiritual world. Angela and I have prayed for this, but we have always known it is not up to us. If God has a place for John Mark to use such a gift, I trust He will restore it if and when the time comes.

For now, I am grateful that for the brief season in which John Mark was seeing spirits, he could count on Angela to confirm and explain what he saw. I can be confident that no matter how the Holy Spirit equips and deploys him in the future, he will be better prepared because his mother was perfectly equipped to help him understand his gifts at an early age.

In those first few years of parenthood, Angela and I quickly came to understand the value of our household koinonia and our unity in the Holy Spirit. That was essential because stress was encroaching on other areas of our lives, particularly on the professional front.

Changing Seasons

Around the time that John Mark was learning to walk and talk, I had uncovered a significant internal theft at the bank. The deeper I dug into the situation, the higher the numbers climbed. As the lead investigator, I felt pressure from all sides—compounded by the fact that it was an internal matter. When someone in a position of trust is the villain, it raises the emotional stakes, the media interest, and the customer concerns.

That being the case, it shouldn't surprise you to hear that various internal stakeholders—Accounting, Human Resources, Security, and Executive Management, to name a few—each brought their own priorities and ideas of how best to handle the investigation. Often, these ideas conflicted. I was reminded of Aesop's fable of the donkey, the young boy, and the old man.

To further exasperate the strain, I had a new boss who had been with the company for only a few weeks when I first discovered the fraud. We hadn't even had a chance to understand each other's work styles before we were thrust into a baptism-by-fire. We learned quickly that we had very different ways of doing things, which fueled some heated discussions and ultimately set the tone for how we would perceive each other for the remainder of my career—a fact that would become important down the road.

At home, Angela undoubtedly was getting weary of my spending extra time at night logged on to the office or getting our evenings interrupted by phone calls. While she encouraged me to find a way to put up some boundaries, she never complained. Instead she quietly picked up my slack—probably more than I realized at the time.

I think she knew that we were dealing with a seasonal disruption and not a "new normal." At some point, the investigation would be complete, and the case would move through the legal system toward a resolution—which it did surprisingly quickly.

Around this time, stress tried to gain a foothold in our second house. The tenants that God had previously (and providentially) provided had another change in circumstance and needed to move after only a year renting from us.

This time, though, a solution came much more quickly. We learned that a family member who had suffered a series of setbacks was on the brink of losing her house and needed a quick, affordable solution. We happened to have an empty house, so we were able to give her a place to call home.

Once again, God showed us that He wasn't done with this resource. More importantly, He reminded us that when He provides answers, they are seldom about us, and more about His purposes, which extend far beyond what we can see or imagine.

As soon as that stress was behind us, my company announced that in the coming months it would complete a merger with another local bank. Work-related stress was becoming a relay race of sorts.

Over the next year, my work days and my mental energy were consumed by all that went into the merger. Some of the pressure came from the sheer volume of work. Some came from the conflicting styles and personalities involved. And still more—too much, I think—came from the fear that set the tone for nearly every meeting and interaction.

I managed to maintain boundaries on my time, but mentally, I was checked out.

This season also coincided with a time of transition within our church after a handful of long-time members and key leaders left. Angela and I both took a more active role in church leadership, but with fewer hands to share the work, we began to wonder—to each other and in our prayers—how much longer God would sustain the church and how He would give us an exit ramp. God assured us—through the words He spoke to Angela—that we were where He wanted us and He would let us know when it was time to move on.

During this time, Angela was elected Chair of the Board of Trustees for the church. General oversight of the church facilities fell to Angela and the rest of the Trustees. From the start, she had a vision of how the building could be used as a resource for ministry. We had already seen how God used us to be a conduit of His comforting presence during an emergency, but what else could we do?

Angela was full of ideas—even some very outside-the-box ideas. We had a kitchen and gathering space that would be well-suited to community dinners (a ministry that we eventually launched). Angela even contemplated turning an unused area of the building into a community laundry room to serve the homeless.

We never pulled that off, but I loved seeing how Angela hoped to use one of her passions—doing laundry—to carry out another passion—serving needy people. She once told me that if money were no object, she would purchase a mobile laundry truck that she could take to places recovering from disasters so that people could at least have clean clothes.

Although that ministry never came to fruition, Angela and I found that the koinonia of our home carried well into serving together in and with the local church (as long as we weren't in the kitchen at the same time).

But Angela's most prominent endeavor as a church leader was how she dealt with the church parsonage becoming vacant after a pastoral transition. She led the church in executing a lease with a local nonprofit that assists people with housing needs.

So instead of putting the church through the expense and stress of renting on the open market, she found a reliable ministry partner that was suited to handling the logistics. As a result, over the years, several families would come to use that house as a transitional home on their journeys from housing-insecurity to self-sufficiency.

Angela and I were partners, so what was my role in this? Primarily, I was tasked with encouraging the congregation to support this endeavor. For many of our established members, this was a new way of doing church and a new way of carrying out ministry. So it took some time and effort for Angela's vision to take hold.

Despite the congregation's numerical challenges, God was still using us—and using the church—to share His love with a few specific people in need.

As this season carried on, the bank merger was complete, and though there were still hiccups in bringing the two organizations together, the stress of the transition was winding down. Just in time, too, because a new stress was on the horizon.

Within weeks of the bank merger, Angela received notice from her employer that the research and development group of which she was a part would be dissolved by the end of the year. Angela had two choices—either accept the layoff or find another role within the company. In response to the layoff notices, the whole group scrambled to apply for whatever openings were available, and in the end, Angela didn't make the cut.

So in December of 2015, Angela became unemployed for the first time in her life. In the season that followed, I got my first real glimpse of how depression affected her.

No Storms, Just Constant Clouds

Like anyone who is freshly unemployed, Angela spent the first few weeks updating her resume, networking, and scouring job boards for good matches. She had a couple of interviews that didn't lead to offers, while also generating a potentially promising lead with a young company where a former coworker landed.

We put a lot of prayer into Angela's job search, and the more we did, the more confident she was that the new company would pan out. She was *certain* that God would open that door for her.

Six months passed and unemployment benefits ran out. Last year's bank merger had netted me a promotion and a raise, and more recently my firstborn had turned 18, ending my child support obligations. By the providence of God's timing, we were able to absorb the financial impact.

Still, Angela started to feel less-than-useful. She was still networking, still being an effective leader at church, and still keeping up with the laundry. But she was more easily tired and often shared her frustration at the slow movement on her job search. Having a preschooler whose energy seemed to grow exponentially each day probably hastened her exhaustion.

It became a season when Angela leaned on me a little more, much the same as I leaned on her in the midst of my professional stress during the previous two years. My memory is hazy, but that might be when I took over the bulk of the cooking duties. Previously, I was the "weekend chef" while Angela covered the Monday-Friday shifts.

Then something else happened. The family member who was renting our second house had her own season of financial difficulty, and she was not able to pay the full rent for over a year. After a year, her husband's pension would kick in, so I knew the setback would be temporary. I did the math and determined that our savings could cover the gap, so that was my plan.

For me, the real struggle was whether or not I should tell Angela about this development. In our household koinonia, management of both our household finances and the rental house fell to me. So I could operate without having to loop Angela in on this detail.

I saw how Angela's lack of employment was already making her feel like she wasn't contributing (a sentiment she often articulated). Yes, she was able to do much for the church as well as spend more time with our preschool-aged son than most parents get, so there were some clear upsides to our circumstance. Still, Angela applied significant weight to her capacity to contribute financially, despite my assurance that her other contributions had equal—if not greater—value.

Considering all these factors, I was concerned that if Angela knew we weren't receiving full rent for the second house, it would push her into worry and panic. I didn't want to have to predict how that would impact her demeanor or her capacity to do the work that God had given her for that particular season.

So I made a difficult decision. I withheld this bit of information from Angela. Some readers might not agree with my choice, and I can promise you that I was deeply conflicted myself. But it seemed like the best way to protect her.

[To not leave you hanging: About four or five years later, when this season was well behind us, I let Angela know about that particular development. Whether it was her wisdom, her grace, or both, I was relieved when she told me that I made the right choice. She also had no way of knowing how another piece of bad news would have affected her at the time, but she was thankful that I kept her from finding out.]

How did Angela's season of depression and jobless-ness get resolved? The startup company that she had been talking to for over a year *finally* had an opening that was a perfect fit for Angela's skills and experience. In fact, it is more accurate to say they created a new position with her in mind. So God did open the door, but as He always does, He did so according to His own timing.

Where Does My Help Come from Now?

The dizzying pace and stress of the first half of our marriage showed me how valuable it is to have a cohe-sive—and flexible—koinonia. Today's needs might not be tomorrow's needs. In fact, our needs will certainly change. It's only a question of when and how much.

Losing a spouse means losing a whole lot of help, without losing any of the need. Actually, it has the opposite effect—losing a spouse *compounds* the need.

There's no great insight to this truth. It's obvious on its face, as any single parent knows.

In the previous section, I shared how our koinonia informed our approach to parenting, to professional endeavors, to church participation, and to work-life balance. These disciplines are all interrelated, and I am still discovering how every one of them looks for me now.

A few weeks after Angela's passing, I met with Pastor Jeff, who said, "I know you're not the kind of person who asks for help, so let me ask you, where is your need?"

At that point, I still had much to figure out, but one point was immediately obvious. I needed people to watch John Mark when I wasn't available. I was happy to let Pastor Jeff know that the church was already doing a lot to address that need.

While Angela's parents have been happily taking John Mark when I have to work Saturdays, our church koinonia has been faithfully covering weekday needs— both sporadic and predictable. It is especially convenient that the one evening I am required to work each week coincides with the church youth group meetings. Because his church friends are headed to the same place, it's easy for John Mark to tag along.

Of course, one of the hallmarks of koinonia is reciprocity, so I welcome those times when John Mark's friends need to spend time here with us. And he enjoys it, too.

Still, there is more to parenting than just scheduling. I need to be mindful that just as I am wrestling with losing my wife, my son is wrestling with losing his mother, even if he doesn't say much about it. I am grateful that others in our wider sphere of influence are mindful of this reality.

Not Just My Needs

In the spring following Angela's passing, John Mark's class had to read a book in which the protagonist loses her father in the opening chapters. The teacher emailed me with a heads-up so I could be prepared to deal with John Mark's reaction.

I checked out the book and read ahead so I could get in front of any reaction from John Mark. He took the book in stride and really got into the story, which gave us plenty to talk about, but not in the way his teacher anticipated. Still, I appreciated the gesture because I don't always know what is going to trigger *me*, much less what will trigger my son.

As spring gave way to summer, then to a new school year, we saw some shifts in our routines. John Mark and I figured out what to keep the same and what to change largely by trial and error. Certain errands had to move to times when I could take John Mark with me. Our customary evening activities, enjoying family shows or tabletop games, changed a bit. John Mark and I are the resident gamers, so we experienced a season of continuity with evening games. We did this less so with TV, which was more Angela's way of unwinding.

All of this change is happening just as John Mark is hitting the middle school years, which adds a new dynamic to our season of transition. If you are a parent, you know that middle school is the time when kids begin to prefer the company of their friends to the company of their parents.

This shift was going to happen no matter what. It's a normal change, and I need to work with it. Even when John Mark and I have an evening at home, he might have a video game "gathering" scheduled with his school friends, and as long as he knows how to manage his time (or heed my time management parameters), I need to give him some latitude.

Still, John Mark and I have found it helpful to partition and protect some time for each other. In the evenings, we make time for a daily scripture reading. In the mornings, we enjoy doing some of the *New York Times'* daily word games together. In the summer months, we spend at least one or two mornings taking our dog on lakeside walks in her favorite park.

I haven't said too much about the dog, but perhaps this is as good a place as any. Abby is a black and white terrier mix that we adopted from a local rescue about four years before Angela's passing. From day one, Abby bonded with Angela, even though Angela had never been a dog person. Really, she bonded with all of us, but Angela was "her human" and the beneficiary of Abby's most endearing affection. Abby is happy to press up against my leg and lean her head on my knee, but she consistently climbed into Angela's—and only Angela's—lap.

It's been heartwarming to observe how John Mark has been slowly taking over the role of "Abby's human" this year. Before, they would happily chase each other around the yard or play fetch (which was more like "keep away" the way Abby plays). Lately, John Mark has been going out of his way to give Abby extra hugs and pets. In response, she has been more inclined to go to him and rest her head on his lap even if I am in the same room.

In this way, John Mark is addressing his own need by meeting the dog's need. I wish I could also get him to show the same responsiveness to washing dishes, but he is a preteen boy, so that is going to be a struggle no matter what.

Dishes aside, I'm grateful that I get to spend so much time observing and participating in these moments. I'm grateful that my schedule and finances—at least for the current season—allow this. It clearly is a gift from God for just such a time as this.

Work-Life Balance

It's impossible to talk about parenting and schedules without talking about finances and work. After all, the reason parents need people to watch our kids is because we have an obligation to work.

At the time of Angela's passing, I was working only 20 hours per week outside the home. (In Part Five, we'll explore how this came to be.) Angela and I had our schedules so neatly assembled that with a little work-from-home time, we could ensure, between the two of us, that John Mark was covered. So one of the biggest worries I faced was how much of a change I would need to make to my schedule and how that would impact John Mark.

Do I need to change jobs (and perhaps abandon writing) in order to cover our expenses? It's a natural, sensible, and necessary question. Fortunately—and I am certain this is the hand of Providence at work—I am in a position right now where I don't need to make any immediate changes. I can get by for at least a couple of years without upending my schedule.

So I made the decision not to make any major life changes (to housing or employment) for at least a year. I determined that it would be best to forgo being super dad and simply focus on being present dad.

If there is a single piece of advice I can offer readers who are in the same situation—losing a spouse and preparing for life as a single parent—this is it: Hold on to your time with your kids to the extent that your finances allow you to do so. (Of course, not everyone can afford to defer additional work for even a few weeks much less a couple of years. So if your financial need is immediate, do what you must to address your needs.)

If you are reading this not as a grieving widow or widower, but as a married person contemplating the future, take steps *now* to give your future schedule a little flexibility.

Recognizing that time is my most precious need in this season, my church has responded wonderfully. I still have plenty of opportunities to serve, including occasional preaching coverage, but the church is mindful that this is not the time to ask me to do anything that would require evening meetings, taking more time away from my son.

The current dynamic will shift naturally—and quickly—on its own. As John Mark grows into a teenager and increasing independence, it will be easier for me to go to monthly administrative meetings or pick up some extra work hours outside the home (unless I somehow start selling books by the thousands).

For now, the choice in my circumstance is clear: rely on my koinonia where I must, be a partner with my koinonia where I can, and model both for my son. Only hindsight will tell how much I get right, but for now, I'll work the adjustments (and the missteps) as they come.

Part Four

Insight and Planning

And this is my prayer: that your love may abound more and more in knowledge and depth of insight …
—*Philippians 1:9*

Lessons from Clothes Shopping

As it turns out, caring for clothes isn't the only science in which I lack proficiency. There is a whole art to buying them, too! And I'm a writer, not an artist.

I can handle the basics, at least for my own clothing needs. I only need to remember a few numbers (two for the shirt size and two for the pants) and a letter (T-shirt size) to keep my clothing current.

By "current," I mean "intact"—not "stylish." Of course you, astute reader, knew that since you already deduced back in Part One that I stopped making fashion choices sometime around 1995, at the height of the grunge era.

A Trip to the Store

Actually, that's not entirely accurate. Somewhere in my suit-and-tie days, I became a fan (and collector) of the Jerry Garcia line of neckties. By the time I left corporate life, I had amassed over thirty. Interestingly, Angela did not buy a single one. The first time she witnessed my deliberation at the tie rack in our local clothing store, she determined that she would never crack the code to my taste in neckties.

This was not a weakness on her part, but a nod to her insight. When it came to clothes shopping, she was fully equipped with both knowledge and insight. As for me, if I happened to be on the shopping excursion (and I usually tried not to be) I was fully equipped to be the pack mule—unless Angela only had a small list. Then she would drop me off at the tie rack and pick me up at checkout time.

I won't even try to describe what was happening when I saw Angela examining three shirts that *looked* like they were all the same color—but apparently were actually different. And I have no idea what would happen when she got sucked into the vortex in the changing rooms. All I know is that was when I got to sit down, rest my arms, and scroll the scores, stats, and highlights from the day's baseball games. Unless it was the off-season, then I would catch up on trades, free-agent signings, and other roster moves.

There was more to shopping than just the art of selecting the clothes. Additional artistry (perhaps higher science?) happened at the register, too. Through some ancient family recipe of coupons, discount codes, and funny-looking store-issued scrip, Angela could concoct a total bill that defied all math and logic.

For Angela, this was a source of utter delight. Her expression was a mix of victory (over the prices) and anticipation (because she just bought two full loads of laundry). Apparently, it's standard procedure to wash new clothes before wearing them. Who knew? Everyone but me, I guess. As a teen, I once spent an entire day wearing a new pair of jeans with the size label still stuck to the leg.

Still, Angela, in her kindness and deference to my quirks, allowed me to wear new socks fresh out of the package. Seriously, if money were no object, I would treat myself to a brand new fresh-out-of-the-package pair of socks every day. Who's with me on this?

Nobody? Okay, back to Angela's story. After all, we've only covered what an excursion to the nearest big-box clothing store looked like. We still have to take a trip to the place where Angela achieved her best scientific (or is it artistic?) breakthroughs.

Next Stop: The Consignment Store

I've been the pack mule on these trips, which is a much more daunting task because small, independent consignment stores simply don't have the basket-and-cart options of the mammoth chain retailers. Sadly, they don't have ties either.

Our local store opened primarily as a children's and maternity consignment store, though they eventually expanded to serve a larger clientele. My memory of the timing is hazy, so I don't remember if Angela found this store before or after our son was born. Still, once she did, it quickly became a favorite. And with good reason.

Children's and maternity is a great model for a consignment store because those are both short-term clothing needs. You only need maternity clothes for a season, and children change size at a seemingly exponential rate. If you close your eyes to sneeze, when you open them again, the child is up to your chin.

I understand how shopping at consignment stores makes good economic sense. Especially when Angela could leverage her store credit (more on that in Part Six) even better than her coupons and scrip from the big-box store.

I joined a few of the early trips to the consignment store, mostly to push the stroller. I was of little help in the racks because all children's clothing pretty much looks the same to me, except for the variance in cartoon characters.

Eventually, the clothes shopping trips began to happen without me. But I still got to hear Angela's enthusiastic reports after each venture. It did not escape my notice that as the years went on, the consignment shop expanded to offer women's clothes (not just maternity) and added racks for older kids and eventually teens. (Allow me a moment to commend their good business sense of maintaining loyal customers by responding to their changing needs.)

So John Mark never outgrew the consignment shop, as I once suspected he would. And Angela would continue to turn old clothes into store credit into new clothes, until the cycle repeated after next week's growth spurt.

However, I was beyond surprised last year when Angela came home from a shopping trip and told me that I should go with her next time because the consignment shop added a *men's* section. This made no sense to me.

Men don't recycle clothes. Men wear clothes until they fall apart. I know this because a) I am a man and b) I have flannels and concert shirts from the '80s and '90s to prove it. The shirt I am wearing right now is an old concert T-shirt from circa 1994. The graphic is faded, and the material is thin and threadbare, but it is still intact after thirty years!

Don't worry—this is just a sleep shirt. Angela always made sure the clothes I wore outside the house were functional and in good repair. If I needed new polos, dress shirts, jeans, etc. she would drag me to the big-box store (but steer me away from the tie rack).

Shopping: Reactive or Proactive?

Even now, without Angela's knowledge and insight to guide me, if something gets a hole or a stain, I am able to replace it. I look at the tag in my pants or shirt and order a like-for-like replacement online. But without an advanced degree in couponing, I'm sure I'll be paying more. So keeping my clothes functional is fairly simple.

The trouble is, I still have to stay on top of buying clothes for my shape-shifting preteen son. This year as we got into the warmer months, I recall John Mark asking me to do some laundry.

"We just did laundry two days ago," I answered.

"But I'm out of shorts."

"How did that happen?"

"These are the only ones that still fit."

Angela *never* would have had this conversation because she was always a step ahead of the need. So we took a trip to the consignment shop, checked to see if Angela had any residual store credit (she didn't), and stocked up for the summer—*after* summer was already underway.

I should probably make a note to myself now to do some back-to-school shopping before summer is over. (Edit to add: John Mark and I pulled off back-to-school clothes shopping with five days to spare.)

This will probably not be the last time I find myself addressing a need in the rearview mirror. I just don't possess the knowledge, wisdom, and foresight that Angela brought to our marriage.

I can anticipate needs in other aspects of household management, but when it came to clothes, Angela was next level. Remember, she was the one who kept lists of lists. Meanwhile, I see the need for new clothes only when I notice the gap between the cuff of my son's pants and the top of his shoe. I'm nowhere near the level of insight that Angela possessed.

Growing in Knowledge

Knowledge and insight—these seem like useful things to ask for. In fact, scripture outright says we should do this. James 1:5 tells us to ask for wisdom when we find that we are lacking. And Jesus teaches us the value of calculating costs and preparing for our endeavors (Luke 14:25-33).

Still, there is a lot more going on in this passage than Paul encouraging the Philippians to seek knowledge, or even praying that they might receive relevant insight. Instead, in verse 9 he prays that their *love would abound* in these qualities.

Love and ... Knowledge?

To our modern Western ears, this sounds like an odd recipe. How could love (full of sentiment and emotions) abound in knowledge and insight (very intellectual pursuits)? In our culture, we understand the head and the heart to be in conflict with one another, or at least to temper each other with tension and resistance. Whole pop culture brands have found success with this very premise.

In this verse, we encounter a reminder that the ancients didn't compartmentalize the head and the heart the way we do. In their thinking, emotions, intellect, and will all belonged jumbled together in an interdependent, inseparable group of qualities. Perhaps we should consider the possibility that modern thinking is jumbled and the ancients had it right all along. Verse 9 is a good starting point.

In the preceding verses, we saw that Paul addressed the Philippians as brothers and sisters in Christ whom he clearly loved. Here, he acknowledges the love that motivates their actions and continued koinonia. It was their love for Paul, *combined with* their knowledge and understanding of his particular circumstance (remember—one of the founding members of the church in Philippi was the jailer), that gave them the insight to assess and respond to his needs in a meaningful, relevant way.

Great! Paul says. Do more of this in even bigger ways!

As recipients of God's grace, we are aware of the love that prompts Him to bestow such a great gift upon us. The more we take refuge in and meditate on God's love, the more our love for Him grows. As John writes, "We love because he first loved us." (1 John 4:19)

This mutual love draws us nearer to our heavenly Father, but not just in a sentimental or emotional way. The more we receive His grace, the more we grow in our knowledge of His love. And the more we draw near to Him—through worship, prayer, and studying His word—the more we grow in our knowledge of His character.

Over seasons of growth, our minds conform more to the mind of Christ, our eyes see other people as God's image bearers, beloved by their heavenly Father and longing for His grace. Our hearts are filled with the love of Christ to capacity *and beyond* so that we might overflow with love for our brothers and sisters, as well as for the lost souls who He has commissioned us to reach.

I am sure many readers have experienced being a conduit of God's grace and love. I'm also certain it continues to be the shape of your lives. That is as it should be.

Growth Takes a Team

Let's also remember that Paul is not addressing an individual in this letter. He isn't even addressing a *group* of individuals. He is writing to the church—the koinonia—the whole partnership of Christians in Philippi. And through the preservation of the scriptures, he is addressing the koinonia of the modern church. Me. You (plural). Us.

Quick aside: I wish there were a simple way to express "you plural" in writing without giving my editor fits. I suppose I could draw from regional dialects, but then I risk alienating the "y'all" readers with my preference for "youse." So please assume, at least for the remainder of this section, that when you see the word "you," you should read it in its plural form.

If we want our love to abound in knowledge and depth of insight, we need our koinonia. Without it, we will not achieve the fullness of love and kingdom service that God has called us to. Yes, we must devote time and thought to our one-on-one prayer and study in communion with our Father. But we must also remember that what we receive from God we work in the Spirit, and through the koinonia. Community is where we *apply and exercise* God's love working in us.

Jesus reminds us that the essence of the law is to love God and love your neighbor. When we read the Ten Commandments, we can draw a bright line between commandments four and five to mark these two sections. Still, they act as a cohesive whole. It is much easier to love your neighbor when you see him or her as a child of God formed in His image.

Jesus instructed the founding koinonia to love one another as he has loved them (and you and us). He further taught them (and you and us) that what we do for the least among us, we do for him. Our interpersonal love is an expression of God's love for us and ours for Him.

When this is how our koinonia functions—bound together and fueled by our Christ-centered mutual love—growing in wisdom and insight comes naturally.

Our cultural caricature of the wise sage is the hermit sitting atop the lonely mountain. In reality, we're more likely to find the wise sage in the trenches and on the front lines, where experience and interdependence abound. These are places where we learn by observation, by compassion, and—yes—by trial and error.

In koinonia, we go to these places together. We teach each other. We err, forgive, learn, and recalibrate as a group. We share our strengths alongside one another, so that our growth and our ministry may be more fruitful than anything we could produce as a mere tabulation of individuals.

Alert and Aware

But we don't go in blind. Despite what our culture tells us, neither love nor faith are blind. They both benefit from being informed. So we pray and we prepare. Part of that preparation is seeking wise counsel (Proverbs 15:22). God can and does use the knowledge and insight of the wise to train up others in the koinonia.

Jesus reminds us that where two or three are gathered in His name, He is present (Matthew 18:20). It is important to understand the context of this verse. It is not about quorum for our worship services. Jesus is speaking about the gathering of believers to plan, strategize, deliberate, and act—particularly in the war room as we prepare for spiritual battle.

Jesus wants us to get ahead of the things we face. He equips us through the Spirit for the work He has prepared for us. All foreknowledge is His. Although *we* are sometimes surprised by our circumstances (and by the means of our delivery), He never is.

We must also be wary that when we seek wise counsel, we do not just seek out comforting words. We don't want to be like King Ahab, who listened only to the false prophets because the real prophet "never prophesies anything good." (2 Chronicles 18:7)

A koinonia built on the foundation of Christ is essential for the proliferation of insight in love. It is essential for anticipating expected needs and preparing for the unexpected. It should not surprise us then to see this truth come alive so vibrantly in the most fundamental form of koinonia—marriage.

A Season of Preparation

Early 2017 marked a change in season for us. Angela was finally preparing to start a new job—one specially made just for her. The stress of the bank merger was behind me, and I was settled in my role in the new-look company.

On top of that, we even bought a new car for Angela—the first car we bought together. We made this purchase out of necessity. My car had died in December, and although I had a small pickup truck to use for miscellaneous projects, it was not a practical everyday vehicle—especially with a job that could take me to any corner of the county on any given day. So Angela picked out a new(ish) Subaru, and I adopted her senior (but still reliable) Toyota.

Back to Normal

With the shedding of stressors and the addition of Angela's job, the change in her disposition was swift and visible. She was very much back to her old self. (I should add that full rent resumed coming in around this time, too, but Angela still didn't know it had ever stopped.) It also helped that, despite our full work schedules, our professional demands didn't encroach on our evenings, so we could build in time for walks at the park and our increasing church leadership obligations.

Angela and I were grateful to serve, and we were grateful to also suddenly be in a position to substantially increase our giving. But overall, church felt stagnant. We weren't seeing new people visiting let alone joining, and denominational politics occasionally crept into local church conversations. To the credit of the entire leadership board, who did not all see eye-to-eye on some of the issues, the team did a wonderful job of not letting the denominational storm disrupt friendships in our pews.

Still, there just wasn't much happening, and Angela and I struggled to find a reason to get excited about church. Perhaps surprisingly, this weighed on Angela much more than me. After all, I had grown up in this church—it had been my home since fourth grade—whereas Angela had been part of the church for less than seven years.

Maybe my long-lived familiarity gave me a sense of residual comfort, despite the reality that the church was not what it used to be. While I wasn't blind to the changing churchscape, I was still optimistic that God would provide a solution for us *within* the church, rather than *beyond* it.

Despite our divergent outlooks, Angela and I agreed that neither of us wanted to sit and watch the church die. Angela began asking again in her prayers how much longer we would be there.

This time, God answered her. He told Angela that we would know it was time to go when I heard something from the pulpit that shouldn't be said—something too erroneous to ignore.

A New Season Coming

Of course, when Angela shared this with me, I had more questions (none of which she could answer). I didn't bother asking if the Lord gave her a timeframe, since He never does. Even if He did, His day is like a thousand years, so I wouldn't be able to work out the math anyway.

The other difficulty I had was that I couldn't conceive what great horror would ever come from the pulpit. Despite our challenges as a church, our pastor's doctrine was sound, and his pursuit of Biblical truth was genuine. If he were to err on an exegetical or contextual point, it would not be an irreconcilable, egregious error. So Angela and I filed that one away for the time being and proceeded with church life with what we had.

One interesting dynamic of an aging church is that as members enter into victory, it is not uncommon for them to leave bequests to the church. Our church had recently been the beneficiary of a fairly substantial bequest, so the church leadership board had some decisions to make with the infusion of cash. We were unanimous in determining that it would be unwise to tuck the gift away for a rainy day, and instead we sought to use it to inject fuel into new ministry ideas.

Angela's community-facing ideas came to the table. The community laundry idea proved to be a logistical nightmare, so we looked for more in-reach options. Community dinners were another alternative we explored. We had the space, a full kitchen, and the funding. But in circulating the idea, we kept hearing that the volunteer pool would be spread too thin. Most of the people who would be good choices to prepare dinners were already putting a lot of effort into various fellowship meals.

Angela was not naturally inclined to anger, but I started to see some passionate emotions in her. At times, she fought back tears when discussing the subject. She was upset that the church could put its energy into feeding ourselves, but not our neighbors. "Why," she wondered aloud, "can't we hold community dinners anyway? We can still eat with them."

She wasn't wrong, but not enough people were swayed.

So with the community dinner idea stalled, the church was still looking for opportunities to steward the funds that we had on hand. We decided to hire a part-time worship leader for our contemporary service. Up to that point, the music was strictly volunteer-led, and all of us were amateurs. So we wanted to bring in someone who had a heart for worship—*and* the skills and proficiency to lead us musically.

Our first and only applicant turned out to be a perfect fit. She brought the necessary musical and leadership skills to our worship team to expand our repertoire and bring cohesion to our music. For the first time in a long time, we had some optimism about what God might be doing in our church. At least, I did.

Angela still tempered her optimism with the knowledge that God had already told us that at some point He would call us away from the church.

Preparing for Changes

Still, we determined that even if our season in that church would come to an end in the not-too-distant future, we ought to be faithful with the time and resources we had in the present.

Around this time, the Lord laid on my heart that He wanted me to preach a sermon series on Revelation chapters 2 and 3. These chapters consist of letters to seven ancient churches, each with their own unique circumstances. The letters reveal much about each church's faithfulness, sins, triumphs, and challenges.

Given that I was simply the lay preacher who filled the pulpit in the pastor's absence, I expected to have two to three years to slowly roll out this series and allow the congregation to wrestle with the titular question: "What church will we be?" Yet, thanks to a mix of vacations, illness, and off-site training, I somehow delivered the first four sermons in this seven-part series before summer had ended.

Since Angela and I started dating, she had always been a sounding board for my sermon preparation. I would go over key points with her, and sometimes she would have insights into the text that I might have missed on a first pass. Other times, she would let me know how important points were landing and when trivial points were getting in the way.

Whether Angela was acting as a research assistant or a test congregation, she was always ready to alert me when I was getting too nerdy. It turns out that not all historical or etymological tidbits are useful in a sermon. In fact, Angela often (but gently) reminded me that they aren't even *interesting* when you hear too many. Who knew?

So as a congregation, we were exploring what church we should be through this sermon series. We had made necessary improvements to our contemporary worship, and the church leaders were still looking for ways to expand our ministry reach. One leader suggested offering the *Financial Peace University* course from Dave Ramsey as a way to introduce people to our church.

Angela and I were excited about this idea—in part because we had just come out of a season where finances were a source of worry. Also we hoped that we could improve our planning and preparation during the current season while we had a decent harvest.

But mostly, we were excited that other leaders were equipped to lead the class, and we could simply enjoy being students.

So that fall, we gathered with half a dozen other families from our church—plus at least that many from outside the church—each week to learn about budgeting, spending habits, and long-term financial planning.

Angela and I were eager to put our newfound knowledge and insights into practice. Even though we never carried credit card balances, we learned that simply using them for routine purchases encouraged us to spend more than we should. We had been chiseling away at the one car loan we had, paying a little extra each month. But when we put our newly acquired strategies into practice, we paid the car off in only a year. We even started holding regular "Budget Committee" meetings (through which we learned that we had very different ideas about how to organize a spreadsheet).

All in all, it was working for our household, and it was working well. But it didn't really do much for the church.

None of the people who came for the class stuck around. Some had long drives; others had home churches. Even the improved quality of our worship services wasn't enough to get people in the door. As the New Year turned and a new summer approached, we were discouraged that we hadn't gained any ground despite all we had done in the previous year.

Sometime in May, exactly a year after God commissioned the "What Church Will We Be?" sermon series, I was preparing the seventh and final message.

The Catalyst for Change

If you're familiar with Revelation 2 and 3, you know the final letter is addressed to the church in Laodicea—the famously lukewarm church. A quick glance or a TL:DR scan that sees only the word "lukewarm," might cause a reader to think the church at Laodicea is simply not excited about what they are doing. Upon closer examination, we find that they are indeed excited, but they are excited about all of the wrong things. Specifically, they are excited about all that they do for themselves.

It is rare for sermon preparation to bring me to tears, but this one did. For a year, we had explored the question of what church we would be, and I feared that I had found the answer in this letter. Angela found me in this tearful state, and I showed her a key verse from the passage: "Here I am! I stand at the door and knock. If anyone hears my voice and opens the door, *I will come in and eat with that person*, and they with me." (Revelation 3:20, emphasis mine)

"Do you know what the Lord put on my heart when I read this verse?" I asked her.

She didn't.

I turned to Matthew 25 and read, "Whatever you do for the least of these you do for me." As you probably know, the context of this well-known (even outside the church) teaching is that Jesus is reminding his disciples (including *present-day* disciples) that when we feed, clothe, comfort, and care for others, we do it *for him*. Angela understood. The community was knocking at the door, and we had to let them in. We decided to revisit the discussion about community dinners.

Usually, Angela's greatest assistance came during sermon preparation. But every once in a while, God showed her something during the delivery. I preached the sermon that the Lord had given me. It was challenging and convicting, and I prayed that it would impact the congregation the way the text had impacted me when I prepared it.

As the Lord peeled back the veil for Angela, she saw pages full of writing, which fell into sets of waiting claws, ready to shred them to bits. In other words, this message was met, at least *somewhere* in the pews, by a spirit of rejection.

This came at a time when increasing turmoil at the highest level of our denomination began to prompt more conversations at our leadership table. Having different perspectives was no longer a matter of abstract disagreement. We were faced with the real possibility that, as a church, we would need to make some hard decisions about our long-term direction.

Still, in the short term, we at least agreed to give the dinners a shot, despite the shortage of volunteers. As a church, we knew we were on a short clock and that God would need to provide a miracle in order for us to survive even a few more years—even apart from doctrinal disagreements.

We spent the next several months ensuring that our kitchen was fully in order. To do this, we tapped into an exciting vein of volunteers. One congregant served on a referral panel in the local court system, and oversaw a pool of people who were completing programs as adjudication of minor offenses. Participants in the program were typically required to complete a certain number of community service hours. Helping us prepare our facility for a community-facing outreach qualified.

I was reminded of how Jesus recruited his first disciples. He called them to *work* alongside him, promising to turn them from fishermen into fishers of men.

Also in this time, I contacted the culinary arts director at our local tech school and arranged for the students to prepare some of the community dinners, which allowed us to stretch our internal pool of volunteer cooks a little more.

Despite these steps, our pastor had decided that he would seek a new appointment elsewhere in the denomination. It was a decision he didn't make lightly, but he did make prayerfully. As leaders, we supported him while continuing with the work we had for the season at hand.

In January 2019, we finally launched our first community dinner. It was sparsely attended, so the people who came had leftovers for several days to take with them. But they also spread the word. Despite our push on social media and in local papers, we knew it was word of mouth that would make a difference. Over the next several months, dinner attendance steadily increased, and we got to know some members of our community who we could not have met any other way.

We also had a few outside volunteers assisting each month through the referral program. A couple of them even continued to help after completing their community service hours simply because they thought it was a worthwhile thing to do. Still, none of this was translating into the kind of church growth we had hoped and prayed for.

As we approached the end of our pastor's tenure, we learned that our worship leader would also be relocating. Both of them served their final Sunday with us on the same week in June. During what would be our final contemporary service, God peeled back the veil for Angela once again.

Clouds on the Horizon

We closed our service with *Revelation Song*. This simple song takes the depiction of heavenly worship found in Revelation 4 and sets it to music. Often, when we sang this song, God would show Angela a group of angels in the front of the sanctuary, leading us in worship alongside our human musicians. This Sunday was one such occasion.

Only this time when the song was over and the service concluded, the angels fell into an orderly procession, walked down the aisle, and exited the back of the church. This vision troubled Angela, and for the first time, we could see how short our time was.

Our full-time pastor was replaced by a part-time pastor, who had previous experience with church closures. We understood the logic behind the appointment. The church was on hospice. Still, Angela and I began to wonder if God was truly asking us to stay until the very end—to be the people to close the church that I grew up in.

In the months that followed, it became apparent that our new pastor did not hold to the same orthodox teaching that we held to, and she brought a theologically liberal interpretation of scripture to the pulpit.

In the meantime, she had asked me to preach one September Sunday about a month in the future to cover her vacation absence. As I wrestled with various texts and prayed for direction, the Lord was silent. Even Angela couldn't find anything to grab on to in the texts and topics I shared with her.

The preceding Sunday morning, a week before I was due to preach, I still hadn't even pinned down the text. Then as worship began, the Lord told Angela, "Today is the day." The day for what? The day that I would receive the signal for our departure. Of course, Angela did not share this with me then—I only learned later. So I was not expecting the signal that morning.

But I recognized it the moment it happened.

"This is not meant to be taken as historical fact." The words hit my ears, and it clicked. After I got past my initial shock of a pastor instructing the congregation not to believe the Bible, I realized that I still had to preach from that same pulpit the following week. That's when God finally gave me the text to use.

At lunch, Angela and I debriefed the sermon, and I asked her what she thought when she heard those words. It turns out she didn't notice them. (I later checked the recording; they were there.) But that's when she told me that she had advance warning that I would hear our trigger that day. Have I mentioned lately that Angela didn't like surprises?

So we got busy preparing a sermon with less than a week to go, effectively a rebuttal that would become the last sermon I would be asked to deliver in that church.

We prayed about when and how we would leave the church. Our leadership terms were up at the end of the year. Angela and I agreed that it would honor God and serve His kingdom to stay on board until our terms ended and to continue coordinating the dinners. If God was going to sustain the dinners, we wanted to facilitate an orderly hand-off of the ministry.

A few weeks later, at our next leadership meeting, we announced the pending resignations of both our leadership roles and our church membership. From there, we began working with other leaders to transition what needed to be transitioned.

The following Sunday, months after the angels made their final procession out of the sanctuary, we sat in worship, and at the start of the service Angela suddenly erupted into tears. She got up and asked me to come with her. We stepped out of the sanctuary and she said, "The wolves are here."

"What?"

Angela reminded me that our previous pastor's final sermon was preached from Paul's farewell message when he left Ephesus, which included this verse, *I know that after I leave, savage wolves will come in among you and will not spare the flock.* (Acts 20:29) That morning, the Lord had pulled back the veil again and showed Angela that indeed, the wolves—hostile creatures from the spiritual world—had arrived.

We decided then that we could no longer worship in that sanctuary, though we did fulfill our leadership obligations and continued to serve dinners through the end of the year. We took our Sunday worship to a new church—one that God led us to by illuminating the sign as only He can each morning when Angela drove past it to work.

A Ray of Sunshine through the Clouds

On our first Sunday in the new church, when it was time for the sermon, the pastor got up and shared—with an obviously heavy heart—that God told him that he could not preach the sermon that he had prepared. He said he prayed and pleaded for whatever last-minute correction it needed so he could preach, but the Lord would not allow it.

The pastor, I later learned, was sure that the new family (Angela, John Mark, and I) who showed up that day would never come back. What he couldn't have known at the time is that obedience in *not* delivering his prepared sermon was precisely the "message" we needed to hear—the means by which God would confirm that He had indeed sent us to this church.

So we did come back. And we heard well-exposited, Biblically grounded sermons. We got to know people, learn names, make friends, and enjoy some Sundays where we could simply worship without having a hundred tasks to do. Both the rest and the relationships were revitalizing us, and we would need them both more than we realized. Angela and I were about to face the greatest storm that we had yet faced.

In December, I heard another wallop of a sentence that would stick in by brain and ring in my ears. Not from the pulpit, but at work—in a meeting with the bank's Chief Operating Officer and Chief Human Resources Officer. Toward the end of the meeting, the latter told me, "With respect to your continued employment, the decision has been made to sever ties."

Did I mention that this was December 2019?

Rest and Recalibration

Life is seasonal. Losing a job just months shy of hitting a twenty-year work anniversary marked a profound shift from one season of life to another. We'll take a closer look at the season that followed in Part Five.

For now, let's look at how those couple of years of prosperity, growth, and preparation inform my perspective on my current season as a new and relatively young widower. First, I am thankful that God used those years to prepare us financially for the unexpected.

Applied Knowledge and Insight

Losing a spouse is devastating and disruptive. Having a budget, a will, a retirement account, and life insurance do not lessen the devastation and disruption. But they at least keep financial concerns from compounding and exacerbating an already painful season. Because the Lord guided Angela and me toward knowledge and insight in these areas years ago, I'm in a season now where I can proceed with prayerful deliberation, not with panicked haste.

In Part Three, I shared how I am finding value in being able to spend a little more time with John Mark in our season of shared grief. Being able to pace myself in this time has other benefits, too.

It takes time and work to change beneficiaries on retirement accounts, update my will, and map out strategies and timelines for future major decisions (which we will explore more fully in Part Five). But the work could be a lot worse. Without a safety net, this would be a season of hasty downsizing, tripling my work hours, and taking early withdrawals from retirement accounts (at a steep cost). My heart breaks for people who have to make such drastic moves on top of the devastation of loss.

At the same time, it reinforces the truth of Paul's words about our love abounding in knowledge and insight. It is out of love for those closest to us that we bother with things like insurance and wills. After all, I will never personally use my life insurance nor my will. And you will never personally use yours.

When Angela and I first had our wills prepared, the attorney explained to us, "You will only need one of these. The trouble is: You don't know which one." So with that question now answered, I can proceed with the necessary adjustments.

Adjusting to my continuing Kingdom work in Angela's absence is more difficult to discern. Who will be my partner in sermon preparation or in ministry in general?

Adapting to New Preparation Strategies

I think of one time when Angela and I prayed over an upcoming sermon and afterward, she told me, "There's one piece you don't have yet." The next day, I received a bit of recent news that filled a gap that I otherwise wouldn't have known even existed.

Even more memorable was the time I was preparing a sermon and went off-roading with a trivial point in the text, and Angela saw an obstacle in my path. So I hit the gas harder and doubled down on my research and outlining. The following day, Angela said I whacked the obstacle with a sledgehammer, but it did not budge.

"Think of it as a stumbling block," she told me. That word led me to a different passage, which served as a signpost to get my sermon back on track.

How can I replace such knowledge and insight? First, I must acknowledge that even though the Lord spoke very vividly and directly through the gifts that He gave Angela, He is still the ultimate source of all knowledge and insight. Though He does not speak audibly to me or show me footage from the spiritual realm—as He did with Angela—He is not silent either.

So when I wrestle with a passage of scripture, particularly one that I intend to preach or write about, I lean on the resources the Lord has given me. The commentaries and reference books are very useful, but I find the most value in bouncing difficult questions off my koinonia. I'm blessed to have a pastor and other church leaders who also desire to get to the truth and who acknowledge that we sometimes need to understand (and teach) it in layers.

Even the studies of Philippians 1 that you have been reading throughout this book have been reviewed by wise pastors, writers, and church leaders whose walk with the Spirit and whose hunger for truth I have witnessed and I trust. If I have stumbled into faulty territory, or if I've distracted my readers with too much nerdy Bible trivia, my koinonia will help me correct these passages. So if by the time this reaches your eyes the studies still aren't landing ... don't blame me.

Still, there is more to my ministry than just the occasional preaching. We haven't yet visited how I began writing and the way that God used Angela in that endeavor. (We will discuss that season in Part Five.)

Partners Lessen the Burden

Within the context of my church koinonia, I find that even though we are not a large church, we are a *high-engagement* church. Our people get involved. Everybody is an active participant in the work of the church. So I am free to serve in areas that suit my gifts and passions. I am equally free to step aside while others serve in areas where they are more suitably gifted than I am. I can slow down for a season while others carry a little more.

Let me just take a moment to say how *liberating* that is.

Further, it is especially critical in a season such as this, as I work through my first year as a widower, still uncertain about much about my future and how both day-to-day life and kingdom service will work. We'll examine the future, to the extent that it is possible, in the latter parts of this book.

For now, I am content to rest on the goodness of God's love, through which He gives us the knowledge and insight that we need, sustains us, and prepares us for whatever future He has set before us. I may not know now how the growth, lessons, and connections that God gives me in this season will impact the future. But I trust that when the future becomes the past, I will be able to look back and see how it all worked.

The Lord gave Angela and me the financial tools and insights to prepare us for this season. And in turn, He is showing me how to make my own eventual departure a less burdensome season for those who follow me.

In love, He connected us with a church community where our gifts are useful in service to His kingdom, and where our brothers and sisters carry out their part alongside us, according to the gifts He has given them.

God foreknew every storm we would face, and He prepared us with knowledge and insight so that we may persevere through each of them.

With the accumulated knowledge of seeing His hand at work in the storms of the past, I can step forward trusting and knowing that He will see me through whatever storms I have yet to face.

Part Five

Listening for God's Wisdom

… so that you may be able to discern what is best and may be pure and blameless for the day of Christ …
—Philippians 1:10

Sorting Strategies

As I continue to navigate the intricacies of caring for my clothes, I remain stumped by the two collapsible baskets that are tucked next to the laundry basket. They've been there for years. I know Angela used them, but I have yet to encounter a need to open even *one*, let alone both. Still, if my memory serves me, these extra baskets have something to do with sorting.

Is Sorting Really Necessary?

The trouble is: The very concept of sorting dirty clothes eludes me. After all, if everything gets washed using the same settings, everything can go in together, right?

I just heard the collective gasp of a subset of readers. I'll pause to give you a moment to recover.

[Please stand by ...]

Okay, let's continue.

To be fair, I generally have to wash the T-shirts, flannels, hoodies, and occasional polo shirts that have been featured throughout this book. So I ask for leeway as you consider that I am probably doing "entry-level" laundry when dealing with my wardrobe. It just makes sense to me that everything goes in the same load.

I'm sure a few of you (the same group who gasped earlier) are now muttering, "I can see why Angela was so quick to take over his laundry." And you may be right.

Yes, I understand women's clothes are different, and they include garments with strange names that I can't pronounce. Perhaps these delicately-named articles require special handling? I don't know. But my wardrobe consists only of things that I can comfortably—and confidently—name. Seriously, I don't even eat *food* that I can't pronounce (with the exception of Worcestershire sauce).

The Unsolvable Puzzle

I'll concede that in some context beyond my basic laundry needs, there is a reason for sorting. I have yet to crack the code, but it's not for a lack of effort on my part. I consider all of the times that I'd just finished a shower and returned to the bedroom with a handful of items for the laundry, and I would encounter several different piles. Then I would freeze.

If I happened upon a live sort, with Angela in the room, she might give me a moment to try to figure out the puzzle before nodding or pointing to the correct answer. I could tell by her knowing smile that she enjoyed watching me solve these impromptu brain teasers.

But I never figured out what made the correct answer correct. I tried matching colors, but it turns out that boxers are "whites" even if they are blue. I tried matching type, but there were socks in every pile. I looked to see if Angela had made his-and-hers piles, but that wasn't the answer either. Once I gave up and put my clothes on the floor where the laundry basket usually sits.

Nope, that was wrong, too.

Wrong or not, it became my go-to solution if Angela wasn't in the room and I had to fend for myself. Sometimes I would hear her sigh when she later discovered what I had done. To her credit, it was always a loving sigh—never an angry one. I'm sure on some level, she thought my struggles with laundry sorting were "cute and endearing," and I am content to look for no further explanation.

Actually, I had one memorable failure that wasn't so cute. It was lawn day, so I had spent a few hours out in the heat getting covered with grass clippings, dirt, pollen, and sweat. At least half of these things aggravated Angela's allergies. Laundry was well underway, and I knew this because every time I passed the back of the house I could smell the dryer vent doing its job.

By the time I finished the lawn and got cleaned up, I didn't have multiple piles to choose from—just a single basket. The usual basket. Sitting right in the middle of the floor. So ... that's where I put my dirty clothes.

Some of you may have seen this sitcom before, and I just heard *another* collective gasp.

I certainly heard the gasp that day. Yes, I had added dirty, allergen-laden clothes on top of a basket of clean laundry.

Apparently, this was cause for rewashing an entire load.

I suspect this episode is the reason Angela ultimately tolerated my putting dirty clothes on the floor (but only where the laundry basket normally resides—I am civilized). She surely recognized that the sorting game was beyond my skills. That isn't to say I haven't tried in recent months to replicate the sorting. (I'm an avid jigsaw puzzler, so I am familiar with various sorting strategies and the need to select different methods in different contexts.)

Observe, Imitate, and Still Fail

During my first few attempts at laundry, I tried some sorting, just as I remember Angela doing it. I'd dump everything out on the floor and start making smaller piles. I never could get the arm movements right, though. Sorting puzzle pieces happens almost exclusively beyond the wrists. Sorting laundry, however, also requires skilled use of the elbows and shoulders.

In fact, sometimes I would see Angela tossing clothes around with such flair and rhythm that I wondered if her sorting should be set to music. On one memorable occasion, her fitness watch chimed mid-sort to let her know that she had reached her swimming goal for the day. Neither of us even knew she *had* a swimming goal.

If you've been paying attention throughout this book, you have probably already concluded that any arm waving that I attempt would be far from graceful. And you'd be correct. I'm sure I would look even more Muppet-like at sorting than I do at the ironing board.

Still, despite my lack of elegance and limited skills, I tried sorting the clothes—at least into major categories (outer/under, colors/whites)—and reached the same conclusion every time. No matter how I subdivided the clothes, I only had enough for one load.

So I'd pile everything back into the basket and put it all in the laundry together. So far, my clothes are coming out clean and intact, so I guess it's okay.

Meanwhile, the collapsible baskets sit idly in the corner, wondering if they will ever have a purpose again.

Perhaps they will. In fact a few years ago, one of the baskets took a side gig for several weeks. Our son had an overabundance of stuffed animals on his bed, and we needed to cull the herd so he had enough room to sleep. So we filled up a basket with the stuffed animals that he was okay with demoting, and they stayed there for a couple of weeks while we figured out an alternate storage solution.

Every laundry day, Angela reminded John Mark that he needed to finish the task so she could have her basket back. Apparently its absence disrupted her laundry operations.

So perhaps there is hope for my lonely baskets.

As for me, I'm resigned to giving up on sorting laundry. It involves a level of discernment that is simply beyond my grasp. Fortunately, as it pertains to laundry, such discernment appears unnecessary for my needs. Not so in life and marriage, though ...

Spirit-Led Discernment

The keyword from verse 10, discern—along with its noun form, discernment—resonates with modern Christians, featuring prominently in the (unofficial) Western Evangelical lexicon. Indeed, they were favorites that Paul (the first editor of the aforementioned "lexicon") returned to regularly.

So what does discernment mean? The Oxford Dictionary offers a concise definition:

"The ability to judge well."

Practicing Discernment

In Christian usage (which Oxford expounds upon in its second entry), discernment is more nuanced and multifaceted. It is separating good from evil. Knowing right from wrong. Distinguishing between the holy and the diabolical. Sorting the things of God from the things of Satan from the things of the world.

Discernment is more complex than just understanding why my blue boxers are "whites." And the stakes are much higher, too.

Though we speak of discernment largely as a spiritual matter (which it is), the word has a mundane origin that is worth understanding. The word discern in this passage (sometimes rendered as "test" in earlier English translations) was a scientific word in the first century. Specifically, it described the process for testing various metals to determine their authenticity and purity. With this insight, we can add identifying the genuine from the counterfeit to our list of definitions above.

It's easy to see why Paul found this to be such a fitting word to illustrate a spiritual matter. The original definition also helps us understand the relationship between being discerning and being pure and blameless.

To be clear, none of us can achieve purity and blamelessness on our own. The good news though, is that if you know Jesus, he has already made you pure and blameless by his work on the cross.

Yes, we all still struggle with sin while we live in mortal bodies in a fallen world. We all sometimes make errors in judgment. This is precisely why we need to be discerning: because we are not impervious to temptation and deception. So discernment is the means by which we seek out the things of God and the character of God, so that our lives may continuously be shaped by the purity that He has already bestowed on us.

Discernment Benefits from Community

This depth of discernment is impossible to achieve if we are going at life alone. Remember the lonely sage at the top of the mountain in Part Four? Let's get him out of our heads for good. Genuine discernment abounds in vibrant Christian community. In koinonia.

Remember: Discern was originally a scientific word. One aspect of proper scientific experimentation is that it is repeatable. Can other testers, in their own labs, with their own equipment, run the same experiment on the same material and get the same results? That's how science knows what is genuine.

It is also how Christians know that we are faithfully interpreting and applying God's word. We use commentaries and other writings that have endured scrutiny and the test of time. We examine scripture for ourselves to determine if new teachings and ideas align with the Bible. Of course we pray so that the Holy Spirit may illuminate our study. And we work out our findings and insights with others within our koinonia.

What happens if we try to discern moral and spiritual matters without any help? We might find ourselves sitting alone, plugging whatever pressing moral question we have into an internet search engine and scrolling through results until we find the answer that most suits our desires, our convenience, or our politics. And chances are, we'd get a whole lot wrong—and not just because there is a lot of contrasting and competing information to sort through.

Consider the circumstance of Paul and the Philippians. Paul planted churches in Roman cultural centers surrounded by all of the licentiousness and paganism that came with being in that time and place.

As if that weren't enough, a group of ultra-legalists followed Paul to several of these church plants to try to enforce adherence to circumcision and other ceremonial aspects of Old Testament law.

So the Philippians and other nascent Christian communities had to deal with the contrasting and competing pressures of permissiveness and legalism. Just like we do today.

Without the capacity to discern the things of God, we can easily get swept into the things of Satan (permissiveness) or the things of the world (legalism).

The Community Benefits from Discernment

In our koinonia, we find not only the wisdom to avoid these traps, but the accountability to live God-honoring and Christ-reflecting lives. Accountability confronts sin within the koinonia that permissiveness ignores, but it does so without the bludgeon of condemnation so often found in legalism. In koinonia, accountability is an act of grace. It is a restorative blend of forgiveness, guidance, and correction. Its purpose is never to destroy—always to rebuild.

As Christians, we submit to accountability because it is part of the cost of surrender. Jesus is in charge now—we are not. If we want to give Him control over our lives, we need to be prepared for course corrections when we go off-roading without Him (sometimes over some nasty terrain).

Also, as members of the koinonia, when we are on the other side of this dynamic, we must remember that Jesus instructs us to forgive not just seven times, but seventy times seven. After all, this is just a fraction of the grace that we have received first from Him.

This brings us to another important question. How do we know if our community is a God-reflecting koinonia that practices Spirit-led discernment?

First, we eliminate the obviously flawed models. Remember the guy sitting alone with his search engine to craft his own distorted theology? If he's charismatic enough, he might someday become a cult leader—one who will *never* encourage you to search the scriptures on your own, but to look to his interpretation alone for guidance.

In Part Four, we met King Ahab, who would only listen to the "prophets" who had pleasant things to say. His refusal to submit to accountability led to his destruction. At the other extreme, if you've been beaten down by legalists, Paul's letter to the Galatians has some encouraging words for you.

At both extremes, scripture shows us examples of bad communities and the consequences that they invite.

Fortunately, it also shows us what healthy, Spirit-led koinonia looks like. They are people who pray for and with one another and search the scriptures together. They care for each other's needs, encourage each other's work, and are motivated by a love for God and love for one another.

Yes, our Christian communities are made up of flawed people, all of whom need occasional correction and recalibration. So did Jesus' original twelve disciples. So did the early church of Acts. So did the seven churches in Revelation. So do you, and so do I.

But please don't take my word for it. Read these stories and study your Bible. If anything I have said contradicts God's word, trust your Bible, not my words.

A Christian community is at its peak spiritual health when all of its members are studying and praying, so that when the community comes together, everyone can be sure.

And this practice is essential in the koinonia of marriage.

Navigating Uncertainty

The week after Christmas, some close friends packed up a U-Haul as they prepared to move from our corner of Pennsylvania to the Raleigh, North Carolina, area. At the send-off, they pulled me aside and handed me a gift card, understanding that being newly unemployed meant being uncertain about everything. We prayed together, and they offered some encouragement by telling me that this may turn out to be one of the best seasons of my life.

It was hard to see how that could be. Unemployment covered about half of what I had been making. Angela was able to boost her hours from 30 per week to 32 to be eligible for benefits through her employer, so we saw a little relief there.

From time to time, church leaders would drop by or pull me aside on a Sunday to hand me a grocery store gift card that they had been asked to pass on to me anonymously. I hadn't asked anyone for help, but I was grateful for the thoughtfulness of my church koinonia.

Meanwhile at home, Angela and I continued to pray and strategize. I spent much of the first month sleeping off burnout, and I picked up a few more household duties. School pickup and dinner preparation now fell exclusively to me. On the professional side, I busied myself with resume updates, joining networking groups, and applying for what seemed to be suitable jobs.

One promising lead that I worked hard was with a local bank where my counterpart was nearing retirement. He and I had a good rapport for the past two decades, so I began meeting with him regularly, with the idea that finding me a role within his bank would allow him to begin succession planning. Unfortunately, the bank did not have a suitable opening, and management was unwilling to create a new position.

So I continued the network grind.

When the World Broke

If you remember the timing that I shared at the end of Part Four, you also know that while I was trying to find my next job, the nightly news was updating us about a novel corona virus (that phrase sounds so retro now ...) first reported in China and ultimately showing up in the United States.

I don't need to remind you what happened next, because you lived it, too. When the networking meetings stopped and many businesses put a freeze on hiring, at least there was one bright spot for us. When John Mark's school closed for the remainder of the school year, we didn't have to scramble to find someone to sit with him. I got to spend a season as a stay-at-home dad.

In the first few weeks, the school had not yet set up all the infrastructure to resume classes online. So instead of sending us (parents) all of the material, they encouraged us to use whatever resources we had available to teach our kids and keep track of what we were doing so the school could count it.

My son is brilliant (it's not hyperbole to say that he is the smartest person I know), but he was still only in first grade, and I was winging it. We used at-home science experiment kits, YouTube videos about geography, and whatever books and activity sets we had on hand. I had no idea how it would turn out, and that was scary. Discussing this with Angela, I asked, "You know what I'm most afraid of?"

"That it will work?" she answered.

She knew me so well.

What did this mean for my quest for new employment? It meant we could slow down and be more discerning about where I looked. To aid us, the Lord started showing Angela what would ultimately turn into a series of visions that would shape the next year plus.

Of course, we didn't slow down on praying about the long-term question of my work. Most people would say being in unfamiliar territory prompts an increase in prayer, and we were no different. So my job situation was a standing item on our daily prayer agenda. I was grateful that the Lord started giving us some feedback, even though we understood very little of it in real time.

A Season of Waiting

God's first response came in early 2020, before the pandemic prompted mass shutdowns. At that point, I was still actively engaging with the local bank where I hoped to land work that was familiar to me.

During an evening prayer, as Angela and I were asking for open doors and direction on my next job, she saw an image of me walking down a path until I encountered an impassible wall. The sides and top of the wall were out of frame. There would be no going around, no climbing, digging, or tunneling.

As was our practice when Angela received a vision, we later discussed and debriefed it. We reached the entirely reasonable conclusion that God was prompting me to wait, for whatever reason His timing required. We didn't think much of it because there could be a variety of reasons for the delay, many of which might have nothing to do with us specifically.

When the world—including our son's school—shut down, we assumed that the wall in Angela's vision represented the pandemic, and that we would simply have to wait out the closures. Within a few weeks, John Mark was joining daily Zoom classes and transmitting his schoolwork through Google Classroom. I was relieved because it took less than two weeks for me to discern that my previous fear was unfounded—I was *not* equipped to teach a first grader.

In the meantime, my networking groups moved to virtual meetings, so I kept up with those. While Angela and I were convinced that I would ultimately land at the local bank I had been engaging with, we had no confirmation so it was necessary for me to explore all options. One night when we were discussing my job prospects and Angela said she was sure that's where I would land, I asked her, "Is this coming from you or from the Big Guy?"

"From me," she answered. Angela never ascribed to a vision or a word from the Lord anything that she wasn't *certain* came from Him. We had learned over the years to ask "Where is this coming from?" in response to new ideas or insights. Angela never took offense to the question. Quite the opposite—she welcomed it because *discerning the source* of our ideas was a necessary part of the process.

This is true whether we hear from the Lord through one of our physical senses, or if He speaks to us in more abstract ways that are harder to articulate. All believers hear from Him in some way, so we all need to practice discernment.

Did we have it easy because of the manner in which the Lord spoke to Angela? In a way, yes, since we got some direct information. But a picture without words still leaves unanswered questions. If you've ever perused the entries for *The New Yorker*'s cartoon caption contests, you've seen how one picture can produce many interpretations.

So while our son was busy with class meetings and schoolwork, I would continue my networking and job hunting. This usually meant having afternoons off to take the dog to the park or spend some time in the batting cage at the local Little League field.

Through my networking group, I connected with another small bank, and that summer a job that perfectly matched my experience opened up. I reached out and had what would be my only formal job interview of 2020. By that time, all signs pointed to school reopening in the fall, so we were praying that God would tear down that wall soon. From time to time, He would show Angela that it was still standing. Through the process of this interview and job candidacy, it did not budge.

Weeks went by, and I heard nothing, until finally I received what seemed like a generic copy/paste email informing me that they had hired someone else for the role. It turns out, the person who first introduced me to that bank had landed the job. I learned that she hadn't applied (since her background was in an unrelated area of banking), but the company liked her and really wanted her on board, so they invited her to consider the position.

I would further learn—about a year later when she abruptly resigned—that I probably dodged a bullet by not landing that job.

A New Profession on the Horizon

By the time September arrived, John Mark returned to in-person learning, and I could dedicate more time to networking, but the leads came slowly, so I still had some unallocated hours in my day.

Around this time, Angela excitedly reported to me that the wall finally came down, but there was still a pile of rubble where it once stood. As much as I was anxious to get moving, I wasn't discouraged by the rubble. The wall was down, and that meant progress. We were a step closer to whatever God had for us on the other side of that wall.

"You're a good writer. Maybe you should do that," Angela said one day—seemingly out of the blue.

Astute readers are already anticipating my next question.

"Is this coming from you or from the Big Guy?"

Angela replied, "From ... me?" She sincerely wasn't sure if this was her own thought or if it was divinely inspired.

I wasn't sure what made her say I was a good writer.

Full disclosure: If you had asked me in my teen years what I wanted to do, I would have told you that I wanted to be a writer. I enjoyed following some fantasy fiction franchises then, and I would have loved to bring similar stories to life. But shortly after graduation, reality took hold, and I got a job at a local bank instead.

I had never tried to write my own stories. I didn't have a journal of writings tucked away anywhere that Angela might have read, so I had no idea what prompted her suggestion. She explained that she based her idea largely on my sermons and my small group studies (even though she experienced those pieces by hearing them, not by reading them).

Once I realized she wasn't suggesting that I should launch the next great fantasy fiction empire, it made a whole lot more sense. She was encouraging me to write the same kind of things I would write for sermons and studies.

I searched the usual job boards using terms like "Christian writer" and "Bible Study writer." I found a few links to niche academic roles outside of my qualifications, but I also found links to some of the freelancer boards. I visited one freelancer site, refined my searches, and discovered a variety of opportunities: blogs, articles, devotionals, sermons, and some of the same specialized academic pieces I had encountered earlier.

Apart from a few business writing seminars in my banking days, I had no formal training as a writer. Still, there were some assignments that required no experience (and offered commensurate compensation), so I decided to take a shot. I pulled together a smattering of Sunday school lessons and church newsletter pieces that I had written into my "portfolio" and created a profile.

After putting out bids on every suitable job I could find (even some that were terribly out of date), I got one response from someone who was building a site and needed articles about church history and doctrine.

I was eager to write as much as he would offer me, but I was still new and unproven (as he undoubtedly saw). The client suggested that he could give me a try-out article; a 500-word piece about a particular aspect of church history. I researched. I wrote. I edited. And I rearranged. I was new to this, so I made sure I had *exactly* 500 words to submit. Not 499, not 501, but 500.

The client was pleased with the result, and he promptly released the agreed upon compensation of $.01 per word. As soon as that $5 payment landed, I took a screenshot, showed it to Angela, and said, "It's official! I'm a professional writer." Think of this as the twenty-first century version of the new restaurant owner who frames the first dollar from the first cup of coffee on the first day of business.

Around that time, Angela saw some movement on the path. Angels would sometimes come by and clear a little bit of the debris. The path was still largely blocked, but at least the work crew was on site.

Gaining Momentum

The client continued to assign me increasingly larger articles, and as I diversified my sample portfolio I soon picked up a few more clients. As 2020 came to a close, I was writing a mix of history articles, devotionals, and verse-of-the-day social media pieces. It was still entry-level work with entry-level pay—far from viable financially—but it felt like I was building to something.

Meanwhile, Angela was beyond encouraging, and she continued to fuel my excitement. In fact, the only "criticism" she offered—if you can even call it that—was when she pointed out that I wasn't taking any days off. Even on weekends, I would find a way to squeeze in an hour of writing each day. She understood the gift of Sabbath rest and didn't want me to lose sight of it.

From time to time, Angela would get updates from the Lord, showing more debris on my career path getting cleared away, but the large stone that blocked the way had not budged.

After the turn of the new year, a friend approached me with a temporary work opportunity helping a local business collect a backlog of receivables. Unemployment (which had been extended twice during the pandemic) had just expired. At 20 hours per week, the collection gig would give me a predictable baseline pay while still freeing enough of my time for writing.

My clients made sure that I had plenty to do. Almost all of my writing in that season centered on devotionals. I was simultaneously writing a year-long women's devotional, a page-a-day inspirational calendar, and a series of week-long devotionals for a mobile app developer.

That summer, an idea that had been brewing deep in my brain bubbled to the surface. With all of the experience I was collecting, why couldn't I write and publish a book of my own? I remembered a Bible study I prepared several years back that explored the lives of the people listed in Jesus' genealogy. I still had the study materials, and after some research, I found that nobody else had thought to craft a devotional around that particular passage.

In between client assignments and my part-time collections work, I began drafting what would eventually become my first book, *Preparing for Jesus.* The timing felt providential. Every few months, my hours at the part-time job were reduced as the backlog of receivables shrank. So I was able to offset the shrinking pay with a mix of additional client work (which continued to grow) and my own devotional project.

In the meantime, I sensed in my spirit that God was indeed putting my work on a new course and that He had closed the banking door for good. So when my old colleague at the local bank reached out to let me know that he had announced his retirement, I thanked him for thinking of me and let him know that I would not be returning to the industry.

A short time after that, Angela said the Lord had shown her that my path was fully clear. Two angels came in, tied cables to the stone obstructing my path, and carried it off.

The message was obvious to both of us: Keep writing. It certainly sounded risky, a far cry from the stable, biweekly paychecks that I had always known. But I had my instructions, and I had the full support of my wife.

Through my networking group, I made contact with a local publisher who could provide editing, design, and other support.

Also around this time, Angela rediscovered an old hobby—painting. She used her free time to watch watercolor tutorials and refresh her artistic skills, which had been lying dormant since her college days. Of course, I was eager to ask her to work out some book cover concepts as I finished drafting *Preparing for Jesus*.

By the time I handed the draft off to my editor in early 2022, I had direction on my next book. Quite different from the first book, next up was a novel, *Coin and Dagger*, which explored the contrasting ideals of Matthew the Tax Collector and Simon the Zealot.

Also in early 2022, I finished the collections gig (which had diminished to one day per week) and put 100 percent of my work time into writing. I spent most of my time on client assignments, and I fit research for my novel into the gaps.

Then one by one, the clients dropped off. I was able to increase my output to my two biggest clients, but I still felt uneasy about having too many eggs in too few baskets. Still, Angela and I had seen repeatedly over the past two years how God used our good months to cover our bad months, so we trusted that He knew what He was doing.

By June, I was ready to begin drafting the novel. I committed to spending about an hour per day on it while filling the rest of my time with client work.

Another Shift

Then I was down to only a single client. And in an even bigger turn, in late June, Angela received a jury summons from the federal court in Philadelphia. Angela was not fond of long commutes or city driving, but neither of us were expecting her to react with a full-on panic attack.

This was scary new territory. After a series of doctor visits and a stressful—but successful—campaign to exempt Angela from jury duty, we determined to forgo medication. But Angela did get connected with a counselor, who turned out to be an ideal match for her needs.

Still, from time to time, her anxiety would bubble up, making it harder for her to participate in social events and family gatherings. The reality that her work supplied the bulk of our income weighed on her by adding much unneeded stress over how her anxiety might affect her job performance. Fortunately, her small, close-knit company was very accommodating and worked with her through these challenges.

For my part, I felt the weight of both doubt and failure. In my mind, if I still had my old banking career, Angela wouldn't have to be burdened by her job, and I could relieve her of this anxiety and stress.

Of course, anyone who wrestles with anxiety knows it is not that simple. Angela reinforced this, reminding me that we have to work in obedience, even if the old way *felt* easier. She also reminded me how much my bank work had consumed me and made me absent even when I was sitting right next to her. She told me that she had no interest in going through that again.

In a way, I felt like the Israelites in the desert, grumbling and wishing to return to Egypt. Meanwhile, Angela was my Moses, encouraging me to stay the course (though with more patience than the original Moses).

Writing full time meant that we didn't have to come up with a childcare solution for the summer. But in July, my last client pulled the plug on a long-term project. For a month, I was down to zero clients until a new client approached me and was able to fill the gap. (I observed then, that since I began drafting my first book, I had zero success bidding on new freelance opportunities. Only when a prospective client approached me did it result in landing a gig.)

With fewer client obligations, I was able to turn up the output on my novel. By the fall, I had a first draft of more than 100,000 words. When I was approaching the finish line, Angela and I prayed for new direction and determined that another part-time job was in order. When I began my search, the first opportunity I saw was an opening at my local public library. I applied there and nowhere else. It just seemed too obvious.

After a phone screening followed by an in-person interview, the library offered me the position. That happened exactly three days after I finished the first draft of *Coin and Dagger*.

So it was a busy fall—starting a new job, promoting my recently released Advent devotional at local stores and events, and revising my novel prior to beta reading.

As another year turned, Angela managed her anxiety well. Her small social circle stayed small, and she often opted out of gatherings. But when anxiety attacks came, they weren't overwhelming, and she knew how to contain them. We both hit milestone birthdays in the summer of 2023—I turned fifty, and four weeks later she turned forty.

She also turned out some new artwork for my upcoming book—both the cover and an alternate piece that I would use for a promotional bookmark.

And just as she had been with *Preparing for Jesus*, Angela was my most vocal supporter in September 2023 when I released *Coin and Dagger*. She was happy to tell anyone and everyone about her husband, the fifty-year-old debut novelist.

If anyone had told either of us that within six months, I would also add "fifty-year-old widower" to my resume, neither of us would have believed it.

Facing New Questions

After four bumpy, ever-shifting years, Angela and I had discerned what God was doing and settled into our new roles. Our jobs would sustain us while God grew my writing work into what He wanted it to be.

Fast forward to today, and I have to question everything all over again.

There are plenty of practical matters to consider. Angela always called this house our "forever home," which was her way of saying, "We are never going through the hassle of moving ever again."

Her absence changes the consideration for me. Not that moving would be less of a hassle. (It wouldn't.) But I have to ask questions now that we did not have to ask together. When John Mark is on his own and I am pushing sixty, do I want to be in this house (with all of its upkeep and yardwork) alone? Or do I anticipate downsizing before then?

From here, I spiral into dozens of interrelated questions about housing, finances, work, and ministry. None of these things exist in a silo; they all affect each other. That's a whole lot to sort. To discern.

Prayer, Counsel, and Accountability

The obvious place to start is, of course, prayer. While I find it easy to pray throughout each day, it is definitely different than before.

Angela's discernment gifts, as I shared in the previous section, were quite special and useful. I miss the imagery that God shared with her (and the blunt statements He provided when I really needed them). But apart from her gifts, I miss the prayer partnership that we had. We had the intimacy and familiarity of being able to pray about anything together. (As husband and wife, all our needs were shared needs.)

I am also reminded how much simply praying out loud alongside another human participant kept my prayers focused and on track. I'm sure many of you know exactly what I mean. How easily does private prayer time morph into a mental review of a to-do list, shopping list, or calendar? I'm sure it's not just me.

So I make an effort to share my personal prayer requests with my small group. Articulating even mundane prayer needs, such as household management and financial planning, not only ensures that others are praying for me in a relevant way, but it also means that through my koinonia, I have access to wise counsel and accountability. Both of these are useful discernment tools and useful in general for the faith journey. And both of them exist only in the context of interpersonal relationships. In koinonia.

Whole books have been compiled on the Biblical teaching of seeking wise counsel, so I won't rehash those efforts here. But let's consider at least a hallmark verse or two:

> For lack of guidance a nation falls,
> but victory is won through many advisers.
> —Proverbs 11:14

> *Plans fail for lack of counsel,*
> *but with many advisers they succeed.*
> *—Proverbs 15:22*

Wise counsel is beneficial for whole nations, for individuals, and for every size group in between. If you read Proverbs as a whole, many of the early chapters reveal how to distinguish wisdom from foolishness. This is necessary when seeking counsel. Remember King Ahab? How much of the reason for his demise rested on the fact that he chose terrible advisers?

Accountability, too, is at its best when it is offered in the context of a grace-driven koinonia. Angela never got angry when I put dirty clothes in the wrong pile, but she didn't fail to correct me either. Likewise, a healthy church koinonia will operate like friends looking out for your best interest (because that's how friends work), not like an employer at review time ensuring that *you* are looking out for *their* best interest.

So my church indeed comes alongside me to aid my walk with Jesus. But where am I going? That's much harder to discern.

I have known since my early twenties that God had placed a call on my life to serve Him vocationally. I spent decades pretending not to hear Him while I settled into the complacency of a job that I enjoyed and performed well. Angela knew this, so we weren't entirely surprised by the upheaval that started in 2019 and ended with an open pathway to writing for His glory and His kingdom purposes.

It's easy to see how we reached this conclusion. While I wouldn't say we were wrong, there's been an obvious shift in the logistics of my writing work. In addition, I've observed a shift in the writing itself.

Though I have never experienced the audio-visual communication from God that was so familiar to Angela, He speaks to me in less tangible ways. For me, His "voice" has always been clearest when I am centered on a task or a project that He has commissioned—particularly writing. Whether preparing a sermon, writing a blog post, or brainstorming a book, He would open the floodgates to my mind on occasion.

Angela knew exactly what was happening when she saw me suddenly grab a notepad or open up the mind-mapping program on my computer. Then afterward, she would help me sort the pile into something useful.

And sometimes, God cuts off the flow of information.

When the Road Moves

After *Coin and Dagger* was complete and nearing publication, I began researching my next novel. I spent the summer and fall of 2023 compiling resources and notes, and by January, I had a simple outline of key plot points in place. I began drafting later in the month, and I had penned perhaps 5,000 words at the time of Angela's departure.

Then that project went silent. It wasn't that I lost my motivation to write. God actually cut off the content of that particular project. What He gave me instead was the book you are reading now. But even this He revealed in stages, purposefully and lovingly.

He led me first to preserve my struggles with all aspects of doing laundry, but without telling me why. When that step was complete, the Lord led me back to Philippians 1 during a conversation with a friend after church. Then He sat me down, put me in "sermon prep mode," and instructed me to break down the text.

I had a sense that this would turn into a book about coping with loss, but it was still very incomplete in my mind.

The next step He gave me was simple—but not easy. He invited me to tell our story. Angela's story. To my delight, He gave me access to memories that I had not reviewed recently because they had been tucked away under piles of more recent memories. Then, to my amazement, He showed me how neatly the chronology of our marriage fit with the flow of the text. Somehow, the story of our marriage became Paul's blueprint for building a koinonia. Or vice versa.

There is no way I could have planned this.

The final step then was to share my takeaways from the text—and our marriage—and apply them now. Not just for myself, but for you.

What happens next, then? A radical change in my work? A new ministry venture? Or perhaps I return to the novel that I put on hold at the onset of this project?

He's giving me glimpses of the answers. Hints, really—designed to focus my prayer and inform my discernment. But those questions and answers are best left for Part Six.

Part Six

Finishing the Race

… filled with the fruit of righteousness that comes through Jesus Christ—to the glory and praise of God.
— Philippians 1:11

Packing and Donating

Back in Part Four, during our shopping trips, Angela and I stopped by the local consignment store. You may recall that she often celebrated her economic triumphs after these trips. In addition to whatever good deals she discovered, she saved even more by using her accumulated store credit.

I understand how consignment shops operate, so I know that store credit is part of the process. But I'm learning that there is a whole art form to this aspect of buying (and selling) clothes that is outside my sphere of experience. After all, I was always just the pack mule (a role that I was happy to fill without ever seeking a promotion).

When it came to consigning clothes, all I had to do was take the bin to the store twice per year. Usually, Angela would pick the bin up the next day, though sometimes this task also fell to me depending on how our work schedules aligned. So my job was simple. I knew the outside of the bin well. (It even has our name on the lid—a completely husband-proof setup.) But there is a whole separate world going on *inside* the bin that I am just now beginning to discover.

The Art of Giving Things Up

Keep in mind that as a man, I wear my clothes until they fall apart. So the whole notion of getting money (even in the form of store credit) for any of my old clothes is a completely foreign concept to me. Still, my hardwired male mind isn't completely impervious to new ideas. Like the AI "learning machines" we read about in the news, I can pick up some tricks and tips with the right exposure.

In Part Four when I took my son to the consignment shop for summer clothes, I asked about any open store credits on Angela's account. (There were none.) I also asked about bringing things in to consign. The owner said that she was still taking spring and summer clothes for a few weeks and that all I had to do was fill a bin, drop it off, and the next day pick up the "no thank yous." This, I learned, is a polite way of saying "the stuff we don't want to sell."

In fairness, I understand that they have limited floor space—and have it allocated a certain way—and therefore cannot shelve everything. Still, I appreciate that the store owner intentionally avoids words like "unsuitable" or "rejection." I see why this store is so popular. Most of all, I appreciate that I don't have to learn "the formula." I can just put everything in the bin and let the store owner make all of the decisions.

Well, not everything. Only spring and summer clothes. To my mind, if a garment has full sleeves or full pant legs, it goes in the "fall/winter" pile for future consignment. For this trip, we'll stick with shorts and short-sleeve shirts. And those not-quite-shorts-not-quite-pants things. I think they're called capris?

I already had all of the too-small clothes that my son pulled from his closet and dresser. All I had to do was to apply my simple pant leg/sleeve yes/no flowchart to Angela's clothes, and we'd be set.

Oh—I also needed the bin.

So I retrieved the bin from its spot on the shelf in the basement, and I found a couple of plastic bags.

One had a handful of John Mark's old clothes labeled "keeps." The other was a bag containing mostly Angela's clothes, labeled "for fall consignment." What I thought was a twice-per-year process was apparently a year-round operation. It turns out that only the pack mule has a semi-annual gig.

About that "keeps" bag: All the clothes in that bag were too small for my son. Still, there must have been some reason that Angela set them aside. As best as I can determine, it has to do with our differences in retaining memories. Of the two of us, Angela was more inclined to hold on to tangible reminders of certain memories. I do this very sparingly.

So I had a decision to make. Do I keep all the contents of the "keeps" bag or do I take a more selective approach? Either choice would honor Angela. I could continue to hang on to all the items she would keep, or I could make use of the store-credit artistry (or is it science?) of the consignment shop.

Measuring Success

Eventually, someone will have to clean up after me, so I went with option two—being selective. Most of the contents of the "keeps" bag were reassigned to the consignment bin. (Full disclosure, I kept a few things from Angela's closet, too. Not too many, but the ones that I am hanging on to are the right ones to keep.)

So most of the spring/summer items came down from their hangers and found a spot in the bin. Now I have no idea what to do with all the hangers. I've been contemplating (since I thought of it thirty seconds ago) finding a way to package them with this book. Buy a book about laundry and get a free limited-edition hanger! That could work, right?

I guess my marketing skills rank right up there with my laundry proficiency.

So I loaded the bin (with no room to spare) and dropped it off at the consignment shop. I had to take a few minutes to set up an account in my own name. There's paperwork involved when you get promoted from pack mule to consignee.

The next day, I picked up the bin and the "no thank you" items. It was noticeably lighter than the day before, so that was encouraging. And within several days, I got an email with a full page-long list of my items now on consignment. It actually worked! I can now make real store credit to put toward my son's next growth-spurt. And I get to do it all again when it's pant legs and sleeves season.

Some of you might be wondering what became of the "no thank yous." Without bothering to sort them any further, or even see what remained, I bagged them up and dropped them off at the local thrift store.

I had to do it that way because despite the jokes woven into this account, cleaning out Angela's clothes was one of the most difficult tasks I have faced in these six months. It's hard to imagine a more glaringly stark visual reminder of my wife's departure than seeing her closet empty.

So yes, I celebrate my success at the consignment store, knowing that my efforts will fund additional clothes for my son. I am also grateful that plenty of Angela's clothes will see new life and good use among members of our community who cannot easily afford clothes.

But with these victories comes the reminder that after the fall/winter pack-up, there won't be another season of managing Angela's clothes. This will be her final victory in the clothing purchase/care/discard cycle.

So too, does the Christian life of koinonia produce a series of results and victories, culminating in an ultimate final victory.

Producing Fruit for God's Glory

Every organization exists for a purpose. Businesses exist to make profit. Children's sports leagues offer recreational opportunities. Charities aim to achieve a particular benefit for others. Clubs provide a social outlet for their members. And secret societies ... well ... I can't tell you what they do.

A Partnership Like No Other

Churches are truly unique. In Part One, we began to unpack the layers of meaning that make up koinonia. When we compare a healthy, vibrant church community with the list of associations above, we see that many organizational aspects found elsewhere also appear in the church.

Yet, there are two functions of Christian koinonia that are unique to the church, and they both appear in verse 11.

The fruit of righteousness.

The glory of God.

No other organization exists for these purposes.

Some might produce fruit in a strictly worldly sense. Businesses strive for profit. Charities aim for community betterment. These are examples of fruit that turns human efforts into earthly results. That doesn't mean they are inherently bad results, just that they fall outside the scope of the fruit of koinonia.

The product of koinonia is the fruit of righteousness or, as N.T. Wright translates this phrase in his *for Everyone* commentary series, "the fruit of right living." It comes directly from Jesus working through us, not from our own effort.

Righteousness itself comes to us only through the atoning work of Jesus (2 Corinthians 5:21). We do not produce it on our own. Similarly, Jesus tells his disciples (ancient and modern alike) that he is the vine, and we are the branches. If a branch wants to produce fruit, it must remain connected to the tree. There is no other way.

So what does it mean for us to produce fruit?

If we think in purely individual terms, we might read in these verses a goal of personal piety. There is some truth to this. As followers of Jesus, our lives should increasingly reflect his character as we mature spiritually.

But these words are not written to individuals. They are written to the koinonia—the body of Christ. That is who we are—a symbiotic whole made of many parts held together and united in purpose by the Holy Spirit. When the whole koinonia reflects the love and power of Jesus, fruit abounds.

Sometimes this comes from the silent witness of our lives. When those outside the koinonia see us united in love, persevering through hardship, and governed by peace, they notice that we are different. We know that Jesus himself is what makes us different. But do others know? Are we filled with the fruit of righteousness to the brim … or are we filled to *overflowing*?

If we keep all that we have been given *to* ourselves and *for* ourselves, we are no different from a private club. Or perhaps a secret society (but we can't know for sure). The unhindered work of Jesus in and through our koinonia will invariably produce more than we can contain. This is by design.

We operate as the body of Christ because we have been commissioned by Jesus to carry on the work that he began with a small handful of followers more than 2,000 years ago. "Go and make disciples," Jesus instructed us when he separated from his earthly body. Making disciples can only happen in koinonia because it is a highly relational process.

Throughout this passage from Paul's letter to the Philippians, we've explored how we grow together, function together, pray together and for one another, and serve together. Similarly, in a healthy koinonia, we nurture one another. We are not merely making converts. We are making *disciples*—full-fledged followers of Jesus, living Spirit-led lives.

A Purpose Like No Other

When the silent witness of our lives—and our shared life in koinonia—opens the door for us to witness with our words, we have something to show people. We have something to invite them to experience because they can see how Jesus' work within us produces joy, peace, and love. They can see how His work through us passes on His grace and love to those in our reach.

In reality, we don't always get this right. Sometimes human priorities, motivations, and pride get in our way. We are an imperfect community made of imperfect people, and we regularly produce imperfect results.

So we do well to remember the ultimate reason that we have been assembled as the body of Christ and commissioned with making disciples. It is all to God's glory. It's not about us—and that's good news. For every church plant or mission team that is transforming thousands of lives, there are hundreds of tiny koinonias touching just a few lives each.

That's perfectly okay. We are not in competition with each other. We celebrate the rescue of one just as excitedly as we celebrate the rescue of thousands because we all serve the same God, and He is glorified in all of it.

Scripture tells us *the heavens declare the glory of God* (Psalm 19:1). Indeed, the vast, immeasurable star field that lies beyond our grasp reveals His grandiosity, His power, and His magnitude. So also does the single lily that without toil is clothed in His splendor so rich that even Solomon's regal robes cannot compare (Matthew 6:28-29). In these smallest of revelations we see God's love, His attention, and His providence on full display.

Our God is the God of great and small. Of many and few. Of astrophysics and microbiology. Each of us who is called to service in the body of Christ has a place in His koinonia, where together we can be filled with righteousness and overflow with grace to bring glory to God.

This is the ultimate objective of our existence as God's image bearers. Even within the smallest (numerically) koinonia of all—marriage—God desires to fill us, equip us, and deploy us so that we might bring Him glory through our marriages.

Angela's Victory Lap

Angela always had a sense that God would somehow launch us into ministry together. Throughout our marriage, we saw pieces of this. Her gifts regularly aided my sermon preparation. We brought more to church leadership meetings as a team than either of us could bring alone. More recently, we served together as greeters in our current church (and I could always count on Angela to catch any mistakes I made when setting the schedule).

But to us, the realization of our joint ministry seemed to be emerging from my growing work as a writer. I would write, and Angela would provide artwork for book covers and promotional material while also cheering me on. Behind the scenes, she made sure that I didn't forget to do things like eat and sleep.

Back to Full Strength?

In the fall of 2023, I released my first novel (and second book overall). I was already knee-deep in research for a spin-off novel, and Angela was working out some early cover art ideas. It seemed like we were right where God wanted us to be. The uncertainty and recalibration of the last four years were finally behind us.

Even Angela's anxiety—which never fully went away—was becoming less of an obstacle. In recent years, Angela's anxiety, combined with her increasingly combative digestive system, prompted her to limit much of her social engagement. She was even careful about selecting which church events to participate in.

Coming into the fall, our pastor announced that we would be addressing spiritual warfare during our adult Sunday school hour in the year ahead. Angela knew it would be difficult to get an even earlier start on Sunday morning, but she was determined to make this class.

"You're going to have to *pray* me into this class," she told the thirty-or-so people in the room on week one. And that's exactly what they did. Week after week, Angela was consistently in class. It was a great source of joy for us that brought with it a sense of victory. It was proof that God was doing something new. Something good.

Yes, Angela's anxiety still surfaced from time to time and her digestive issues did not disappear, but the Lord gave her the grace to participate despite these challenges. All to His glory. The congregation celebrated with us and continued to encourage her weekly.

Also that fall, our small Bible study group had grown to a size where it became necessary to branch into two groups. Because of her anxiety, Angela had not been participating in small groups for over a year. But with a new smaller group, she resumed participating.

Meanwhile, back in Sunday school, our pastor offered an important word of preparation to the class. He shared that in his experience, he had never taught a class on spiritual warfare without seeing the church come under spiritual attack.

This informed how we prayed for the church each week—especially for Angela because her gifts would prove insightful in the midst of spiritual warfare. In fact, she began to see a gathering cloud over the church when we would pray—not a friendly cloud bringing life-nourishing rain, but a hostile dark cloud.

Over time, Angela saw a funnel drop from the cloud and wind its way toward the church. This was not a wide-mouthed twister that rips through whole neighborhoods and flattens entire ZIP codes. It was a precision operation, a thin tendril that narrowed to a fine point as it pierced the roof of the church and aimed for a singular spot in the sanctuary.

Despite the precision of the attack, Angela's vision of it was less-than-precise. At least, she could not discern *where* in the sanctuary it touched down. It is not surprising that the Holy Spirit would withhold that detail. If we could have identified such an attack as affecting a particular person or function, it would be too easy for unhealthy human judgments and tactics to work their way into our prayers and actions.

Instead, we focused on the larger truth. What affects *one* of us in the koinonia affects *all* of us. We understood a spiritual attack on one member as an attack on the whole church, and that is how we prayed. As a body, this emboldened us to turn to one another for prayer for all our needs. Whether people were facing illness, family challenges, major decisions, or temptation, we asked the rest of the koinonia to lift us up.

This went on for months, without any update to Angela's vision. At no point beyond this did she see the funnel move or strike beyond its initial touchdown. Nor did we as a church experience any discord, conflict, or scandal that would have made us all say, "That was it." Over time, Angela's vision moved to the back of our minds as we continued with our weekly gatherings and lessons.

Resurgent Momentum

Meanwhile at home, the release of my first novel was at the top of our minds. Shortly before the book's release, I launched my new website and blog and expanded my social media presence. I also committed to one in-person event per month in an effort to get the book off to a good start.

At every step, Angela was alongside me, telling everyone in her sphere of influence where to find me and my books, which she did with genuine joy. Her social media posts were full of fun. Her reports of conversations with coworkers came across with excitement.

To us, these were not my books. This was not my writing career. These were *our* books, and this was *our ministry*. The only reason that I started writing was because Angela first encouraged me to do so. Then she persevered with me through financial ups and downs because she was certain of the call God placed on our lives, our marriage, and our koinonia—and she had no intention of abandoning that call.

Still, her participation in promoting my books was not something that she did out of resigned duty or compelled obligation. She *wanted* to do it. Her anxiety never once slowed her down. To see her in this context, it would have been impossible for an observer to catch even a hint of anxiety in her. She was completely in her element, even though it was not an element she ever would have chosen for herself.

With the Christmas season, Angela was more engaging than she had been in recent years. While she didn't suddenly transform into an extrovert, she didn't back out of social and family events. As long as she chose her food carefully, her super-selective digestive system didn't derail her participation. Though her anxiety wasn't gone, there seemed to be certain aspects of her life—and our shared life—that were insulated from its effects.

Approaching the new year, we still had a lot of momentum. I was invited to promote my book on a radio show and podcast. This was a new experience for me, but it still gave Angela something to share with her friends and colleagues.

I can't overstate how much encouragement I received simply knowing that I had Angela's full—and joyful—support. Still, she also served as a useful gauge.

Remember the discernment we discussed back in Part Five? If an opportunity to do something new or different didn't seem right to Angela, she would say so. An acquaintance was launching a new Internet radio presence and offered me my own show. This would have been a considerable investment of both time and money.

The more we prayed, the clearer it became that this was not a door that God intended to open for us. We didn't discern anything troubling with the radio opportunity. It simply wasn't the place God wanted us to be.

As we prayed through our personal ministry opportunities, we also continued to pray for our church and its direction as we wrapped up the Christmas season and resumed our classes on spiritual warfare.

In early January, a friend from church, whose gifts were similar to Angela's, suggested that we get together for a dedicated prayer time. We had discussed the cloud and the funnel with him. Sometimes, the Lord would show him things that confirmed what He revealed to Angela.

Let's take a quick aside to address the importance of confirmation. None of us is given *all* the spiritual gifts. The Lord distributes them across the body so that we can work together for His glory. Furthermore, He uses members of the body to keep each other in check and on track in our work.

Confirmation of our plans and steps can sometimes be as direct as a vision (or a shared vision), or it might come from an unprompted word of wisdom. And it often happens when you take a step toward where you believe the Lord is leading you and see how He responds. Perhaps the most important thing to understand is that confirmation is a community endeavor. God uses our wise counsel—our koinonia—in this process.

Passing a Signpost

Our friend visited one evening, and we prayed. We had no new revelations about the church, but after we prayed, our visitor did something unexpected. He offered to wash our feet. Of course, we were familiar with the famous passage in John's gospel where Jesus washed the disciples' feet at the Last Supper. And I had participated in foot washing at various retreats and training sessions over the years. But this was different.

This was in our house.

And it was just us.

Still, we couldn't argue with what was clearly a prompt by the Holy Spirit, so our friend washed our feet. I cannot recall everything that he said, but I do remember him speaking of a spirit of forgiveness within Angela. I recalled the "bowels of mercy" that we explored in Part Three. Maybe my nerd brain was cleverly connecting forgiveness with Angela's ongoing digestive troubles. I considered that the source of her digestive distress might even be a spiritual attack, perhaps meant to inhibit her acting on compassion and forgiveness.

It is outside the scope of this writing to examine the particulars of the past wounds Angela was working to forgive. Nor do we need those particulars because just about everyone—without thinking too long or hard—can recall people and events from *our own* pasts that we need to forgive. In this way, Angela was no different from any of us.

As the evening wrapped up, Angela and I both sensed that God was doing something—and that it would be big. We didn't sense that we had stepped onto a new path, but that perhaps we had crossed a mile marker of some kind and the road beneath us was suddenly a little better maintained, with brighter markings and fewer potholes.

We didn't know at the time that within three days, Angela's digestive trouble would prompt a trip to the emergency room.

Sunday morning, Angela woke with severe abdominal pain—not the I-ate-something-disagreeable pain, but a far sharper sting. The winter weather was making a mess of the roads, so Angela was already prepared not to make the trip to church and follow along on the livestream instead.

She also knew the winter roads would not prevent me from making the trip. Very few things will keep me from getting to church on a Sunday morning. However, the need to take my wife to the emergency room was one of those things. So we braved the snowy roads to get to the local hospital and arranged for Angela's parents to meet us there to pick up John Mark.

The emergency room was quiet, and triage went quickly. Upon hearing Angela describe her symptoms, the doctor ordered some imaging. He said it sounded like diverticulitis, but he had never seen that condition in someone so young, so he expected imaging to reveal some other cause.

The results showed that the doctor's first inclination was correct. Angela had developed diverticulitis. Fortunately, with some dietary adjustments, this was completely manageable. I had already discovered dozens of ways to prepare chicken and rice and keep it interesting, so we reasoned that it wouldn't be hard to make further adjustments given the number of food restrictions we were already managing.

However, that wasn't the only noteworthy item to show up in Angela's imaging results. The doctor also identified a nodule on her adrenal gland. Assessing the nodule was outside the scope of our emergency room visit, so Angela scheduled follow-up appointments for both the nodule and the digestive developments.

She had to heal from the current issue first, so over the next couple of weeks as her digestive pain decreased, she busied herself researching everything she could about the nodule on her adrenal gland.

The Panic Button

As a trained biologist, Angela was better-equipped than the average layperson at using Internet searches to understand her medical situation. It helped that she could use more complex terminology than most of us. During one such research session, Angela looked up from her phone and abruptly declared, "I think I found my panic button."

I was eyeballs deep in whatever I was reading at the moment, so I asked her to back up and start over.

"The nodule on my adrenal gland," she said. "It could *literally* be my panic button."

It is impossible to overstate Angela's excitement over this discovery. Even as she was navigating digestive troubles, she eagerly anticipated finally getting some answers about her panic attacks. So she continued her research in order to be as fully informed as possible heading into her appointments.

Not all of her armchair medical research produced this kind of enthusiasm. Usually, it played out more like the scene that happened a couple of weeks later, toward the end of January. While looking into a mild pain in a new place (unrelated), Angela prompted a conversation that we have had a handful of times over the years.

She opened with, "I think I found how I'm going to die."

"The worst case scenario isn't the only possible scenario," I answered. "You're not going to die. At least not any time soon."

"You don't know that."

"Sure I do."

"How can you know that?"

"Because God still has work for us to do. I've already started my next book, and you need to paint the cover."

If you read this as a lighthearted exchange bordering on banter, you picked up the mood correctly. This was a recurring conversation in our house (though the book cover angle was unique to this iteration), and it captures the essence of how we operated. Angela ensured that we considered even the worst possible outcomes while I stubbornly refused to yield my optimism.

Besides, I sincerely believed that our koinonia was destined for a long and fruitful future. God was just beginning to build this ministry of writing, and He had shown Angela how she fit into the plan. This was *our thing* that we were doing in partnership, and God had ordained it. How could it be anything but long term?

Whatever momentary pain prompted that brief conversation went away. Angela's digestive issues improved, and her follow-up appointments indicated that she was on a good course. Everything had returned to normal; I was writing and Angela was painting. She had a small uptick in panic attacks, but at least answers were on the horizon. Meanwhile, the church continued to cover both Angela's health and our shared work with prayer.

Then in early February, a flu that was making its way around our area found its way to Angela.

She stayed home from work on Thursday and Friday. Angela always had a hard time shedding colds quickly, so she anticipated needing more than just the weekend. Plus, it was February so she was monitoring the forecast, which called for snow starting late Monday. Angela mapped out her plan. Monday she would take another sick day if necessary. Otherwise, she would work from home. She already planned to work from home on Tuesday because of the anticipated weather, then return to normal for the back half of the week.

The next few days went as expected, Angela was miserable and rested a lot, but we didn't see anything that suggested the flu wouldn't run its course.

Saturday night after we prayed, Angela shared that while I was praying for her recovery, she saw a handful of tiny demons bouncing off her like popcorn. She was warmer than usual in that moment, but not alarmingly so. We were confident that whatever sneak attack the enemy was attempting through this illness had been thwarted, and we rested in the encouraging reminder that God was at work in the situation.

By the morning, Angela seemed to have improved. Her temperature was back to normal, and her other symptoms had begun to subside. She was still weak and tired after a few days of fighting off the flu, but that was to be expected.

I shared the latest update with the church during our Sunday school hour—even the piece about the demon sneak attack. So the church continued to pray, not only for Angela's health, but also with the awareness that the enemy was not going down without a fight.

That afternoon, I was scheduled to visit a nearby retirement community where I would be preaching later that month. This was a new outreach partnership for our church, so I wanted to observe how another partner church conducted the worship services and get the lay of the land before launching our ministry.

Angela asked me to skip the visit and stay home instead. I was reluctant to back out of a commitment, and Angela knew this but insisted anyway. It was Super Bowl Sunday, and I would be getting together with friends that evening, so she reasoned that she didn't want me gone the whole day. "Besides," she added, "the services at the retirement home will go fine. You've done this before."

So I did as she asked and simply spent the afternoon helping her rest. I soon realized that I really needed the rest, too. (Angela no doubt saw this, but she appealed to reasons that she knew I would respond to instead.)

That evening, as planned, John Mark and I spent the first half of the big game gathering with friends from church. Angela texted as normal to make sure John Mark had enough to eat (and not just junk food) and gauge when we would be coming home. She kept herself occupied with her normal slate of shows.

I came home to find her resting on the couch, in her normal spot, doing her normal thing. We got John Mark off to bed as normal. Then Angela went to bed as normal. Her plan was on track.

The next morning, we put John Mark on the bus, and Angela was moving about a little more than she had in recent days, ready to have her final recovery day before her work-from-home Tuesday.

Then halfway through my workday, the plan changed when Angela called me to say, "I need to go to the hospital. I just passed out."

A Legacy and a Blank Page

"How will you know when the book is done?"

A friend asked this question a few months ago when I told him about the premise and structure of this book. Considering that I wrote portions of this book in real time without the benefit of hindsight, it was a reasonable question. But when we consider our life's work—particularly our kingdom work for God's glory—how do *any* of us know when the work is done?

"I don't know now, but I'll know when I get there," I answered.

Declaring Victory

I was speaking about this book, but the same truth applies to life. Angela planned to return to work on Tuesday, February 13. She planned to paint a book cover for a new book that I planned to write. These plans were in place and moving ahead. None of them came to fruition.

Yet somehow, Angela's kingdom work was done. She had finished the race, kept the faith, and entered into victory. And she had produced more fruit than I could have realized at the time.

Nine days after Angela's departure, we gathered in our church to say final goodbyes. Family members traveled across the country. We saw friends and co-workers from all eras of Angela's life. Many of my own colleagues, past and present, came out. I met dozens of people from Angela's early years for the first time. The church sanctuary was more packed than it was on Christmas Eve. It was standing room only, and even that might have run out. I distinctly remember the look of awe on my father-in-law's face. He was overwhelmed with the outpouring of love for Angela. He had never seen such a large funeral gathering.

Even though Angela wasn't an extrovert who gathered people to herself in vast numbers, the numbers were present that day. And we saw in that crowd the fruit of touching even a single life at a time, benefiting one person for a season, making a small difference in one small space. Over a lifetime—even a lifetime cut way too short by human standards—the harvest can indeed be plentiful. All to God's glory.

People we hadn't spoken to in years shared heartfelt memories of the good that Angela had done in their lives. Then Pastor Jeff shared a vibrant, gospel-centered reflection of Angela's impact during her four years at our church. After the service, my father-in-law commented, "You can tell the pastor really knew Angela and didn't just pull something out of a binder."

Turning Pages

Now as I reflect on Angela's victory and the Lord's harvest of her fruit, I wonder—prayerfully—what comes next. The Lord hasn't been showing me much in recent months as He has been keeping me focused on this project. This book, in a way, completes Angela's work. It provides a means for her life to continue to testify to God's glory and produce fruit for His kingdom. It's the final work of our koinonia.

Yet even after this book is released and I have a season of promotion (you can still get a free hanger), my work will still continue. But what will it look like? Do I return to the unfinished book that I put on hold when I lost Angela? I would like to, and if God wills it (which I have reasons to believe He will), I will do so.

Beyond that? I don't know. What I do know is that I have no desire to return to the complacency of routine that defined my life when the Lord first brought Angela and me together.

I also know that whatever He chooses for me to do, He will not let me do alone. He has made me part of the koinonia of my local church so I have partners in prayer, in ministry, in encouragement, in accountability. Might He bring other collaborators into my sphere—even if only for a season—for the purpose of completing specific assignments? Possibly.

I mentioned in the introduction that I wasn't able to offer answers to your grief, your marriage, or your ministry questions, but that we might find some answers if we take this journey together. For my part, I believe I have found a couple answers—and some useful questions for the next steps on my journey.

Whether you are looking for strategies for your marriage, comfort in your grief, discernment in your search for a church, or guidance for your ministry, I pray that something in these pages was encouraging or helpful to you.

I don't know what goes on the next page in my story, but I know I have more chapters to write. More importantly, I know that the One who directs my work will continue to direct me to the right partners for carrying out that work.

Your journey also remains unfinished and open-ended. I am grateful to have partnered with you throughout these pages, and I pray that He who began a good work in you (plural) will carry it on to completion.

Acknowledgments

First, I owe all gratitude and glory to God, my Rock; Jesus, my Redeemer; and the Holy Spirit, my Strength. Words cannot describe how You have powerfully and lovingly sustained me through the most difficult season of my life.

To the individuals on my list, you are far too numerous to name, as the preceding pages reveal. I am grateful for all of the family and friends who stepped up and stepped in to offer comfort and support to John Mark and me in our time of need. Each one of you has made a bigger difference than you know.

Thank you to the teams at Bucks County Free Library, KCAS Bio, and Faith Christian Academy for all the ways that you supported us during our time of sorrow, uncertainty, and transition.

As always, thanks to Jennifer and the rest of the Bright Communications team for all your work on this project to help make this book a reality.

Finally, thank you to my faith family at Christ Community Bible Church, for sharing this journey with John Mark and me and for living out the fullness of Biblical, Christ-centered koinonia alongside us.

About the Author

Jac Filer is a lifelong resident of Bucks County, Pennsylvania, where he presently lives with his son and his dog. Since 2020, he has been enjoying a second career as a writer. Jac started writing as a freelance contributor to multiple Christian blogs, websites, and devotional apps before turning his attention to writing books. Jac published his first book, *Preparing for Jesus*, in 2022. The following year, he released his first novel, *Coin and Dagger*.